THE ACA LEGAL SERIES

Volume 10

"LEGAL ISSUES IN CLINICAL SUPERVISION"

THE ACA LEGAL SERIES:

Series Editor: Theodore P. Remley, Jr., JD, PhD

Volume 1 ***Preparing for Court Appearances***
Theodore P. Remley, Jr., JD, PhD

Volume 2 ***Documentation in Counseling Records***
Robert W. Mitchell, ACSW

Volume 3 ***Law and Management of a Counseling Agency or Private Practice***
Ronald K. Bullis, JD, MDiv

Volume 4 ***Counseling Minor Clients***
Mark M. Salo, MEd
Stephen G. Shumate, JD, MS

Volume 5 ***The Counselor as Expert Witness***
William J. Weikel, PhD
Paula Richardson Hughes, JD

Volume 6 ***Confidentiality and Privileged Communication***
Gibbs L. Arthur, Jr., MEd
Carl D. Swanson, JD, EdD

Volume 7 ***Legal Issues in Marriage and Family Counseling***
Patricia Stevens-Smith, PhD
Marcia M. Hughes, JD

Volume 8 ***The Danger-to-Self-or-Others Exception to Confidentiality***
C. Emmanuel Ahia, JD, PhD
Dan Martin, JD

Volume 9 ***Third-Party Payments***
J. Steve Strosnider
John D. Grad, JD

Volume 10 ***Legal Issues in Clinical Supervision***
M. Janelle Disney, PhD
Anthony M. Stephens, JD

Volume 11 ***Legal Issues in Licensure***
Donald Anderson, EdD
Carl D. Swanson, JD, EdD

Volume 12 ***Avoiding Counselor Malpractice***
Robert L. Crawford, JD, EdD

THE ACA LEGAL SERIES

Volume 10

"LEGAL ISSUES IN CLINICAL SUPERVISION"

M. Janelle Disney, PhD
Anthony M. Stephens, JD

Series Editor
Theodore P. Remley, Jr., JD, PhD

AMERICAN COUNSELING ASSOCIATION

Legal Issues in Clinical Supervision

10 9 8 7 6 5 4 3 2 1

American Counseling Association
5999 Stevenson Avenue
Alexandria, VA 22304

Director of Communications
Jennifer L. Sacks

Acquisitions and Development Editor
Carolyn Baker

Production/Design Manager
Michael Comlish

Copyeditor
Lucy Blanton

Library of Congress Cataloging-in-Publication Data

Anthony M. Stephens
Legal issues in clinical supervision / M. Janelle Disney, Anthony M. Stephens
p. cm.
Includes bibliographical references.
ISBN 1-55620-128-1
1. Mental health counselors—Legal status, laws, etc.—United States. 2. Mental health counselors—Supervision of—United States. 3. Mental health counseling—Moral and ethical aspects. 4. Respondeat superior—United States. I. Stephens, Anthony M. II. Title.
KF2910.P753D57 1994
344.73'044—dc20 93-36194
[347.30444] CIP

Contents

Acknowledgements

We want to thank those people who assisted and supported us in writing this monograph. Special thanks go to Shannon Monceaux who patiently and laboriously typed the revisions of the text. We also thank Theodore P. Remley, Jr., for initially providing us with the opportunity for this work. His support and suggestions have been most helpful. We thank all of those individuals who provided valuable information, especially the staff at the University of Alabama Law School Library. Finally, we express love and gratitude to our dearest supporters—Richard, Adrienne, Ruth, and Sara.

Biographies

M. Janelle Disney is a counselor educator who is an associate professor in the Department of Psychology at McNeese State University in Lake Charles, Louisiana. She is also a licensed professional counselor who maintains a private practice. Dr. Disney received her PhD in educational psychology with a concentration in counseling from the University of Alabama. She has served as secretary of the Louisiana Psychological Association, president of the Southwest Louisiana Psychological Association, and president of the Louisiana Association for Counselor Education and Supervision; and she is serving as treasurer for the newly formed Louisiana Association for Marriage and Family Counseling. Additionally, Dr. Disney has served as the director of counseling, scholarships, and testing at McNeese; has presented seminars on laughter therapy in Louisiana and Texas; and has appeared frequently on KPLC-TV, Lake Charles, and WAFB-TV, Baton Rouge, presenting information related to mental health.

Anthony M. Stephens is not only a practicing attorney but also an educator in the public school system in Lake Charles, Louisiana. He has taught social studies at the secondary level for 10 years. Since receiving his Juris Doctorate from Louisiana State University in 1988, he has maintained a general practice of law with emphasis in the fields of domestic law and legal research. Additionally, he provides workshops and seminars on legal aspects of the mental health professions.

Dr. Disney and Mr. Stephens are married and have four children.

Theodore P. Remley, Jr., Series Editor, is Executive Director of the American Counseling Association. Immediately prior to assuming this position, Dr. Remley was chair of the Department of Counselor Education at Mississippi State University in Starkville. He holds a PhD from the Department of Counselor Education at the University of Florida in Gainesville and a JD in law from the Catholic University of America in Washington, DC.

Preface

Recent decades have been marked by a tremendous expansion of the role played by mental health professionals in the legal process. It is safe to say that the modern justice system, as it has evolved in recent years, could not function without significant participation by mental health professionals. The roles of these professionals vary but generally take the form of expert testimony in cases involving personal injury, divorce, child custody, and child or spouse abuse. Counselors are being sought in growing numbers to provide court-directed services, including divorce mediation and counseling where abuse has been established. In addition to mental health clinicians, mental health professionals involved in the scientific and research oriented disciplines also have begun to be sought by the courts for their expertise and have had a great influence upon the legal process.

This relationship, however, has not been a one-way street. Just as the mental health professions have come to influence many aspects of law and legal process, the law has also had a significant influence on many aspects of counseling. Today, more than at any time in the past, counselors are being required to practice according to the rapidly changing letter of the law. The once strictly ethical issues such as confidentiality and limits of the counselor/client relationship have now become legal mandates. With the ever-growing specter of malpractice suits, it is clear that no one in the counseling profession can afford to be ignorant of the many statutes and court decisions that regulate the profession.

Where ethical standards represent the ideal counselor behavior in providing for clients, laws that pertain to the counseling profession represent the *acceptable limits* of counselor behavior. Knowledge of both laws and ethics is important because the legal system has used ethical standards in creating laws. In fact, the ethical code for counselors in some states has been incorporated into the law, making any breech of this code a cause for state disciplinary action. Thus ignorance of the laws related to the counseling profession, and ignorance of ethical standards in some states, is at best inadvisable and at worst a prescription for disaster in our "suit happy" nation.

Suits filed against mental health practitioners have increased in the past several decades. In turn, insurance companies have increased premiums for malpractice insurance. For example, in 1978 counselors paid an annual premium of $75; by 1992 the annual premium had increased to $350. Premiums differ for individuals in the various mental health professions, with psychiatrists paying some of the highest rates, social workers paying some of the lowest rates, and professional counselors falling between the two. There may be several reasons for these differences. The practice of psychiatry is a specific medical specialty that utilizes drug therapy, electroconvulsive therapy, and involuntary commitment. Individuals involved in these procedures may be more prone to dissatisfaction with treatment, hence more likely to sue. The "deep pockets" theory has also been suggested. Higher rates for services generally indicate a greater personal income and, it is believed, more money to be awarded in a suit. Because psychiatrists usually charge the highest fees of those in the helping professions, they may be named more frequently in malpractice suits, which in turn causes their insurance costs to soar. In any event, counselors and counselor supervisors are well advised to become familiar with all behaviors that could create legal liability regardless of being less likely to be involved in a suit than those in other mental health professions. In addition, liability insurance is essential for clinical supervisors and their supervisees and is best purchased from the same company.

Legal literature addressing the special role and behaviors of the clinical supervisor is scarce, as are cases related to this practice. Therefore, cases decided in related fields, such as the supervision of medical interns or assistants, must be considered in predicting how courts might rule on suits involving clinical supervisors. The legal system frequently borrows from related professions in fashioning policies and procedures and in making decisions if no rules exist regarding a matter such as clinical supervision.

The authors' objective in this monograph is to inform clinical supervisors of some of the legal principles involved in their work and to aid them in acquiring knowledge to help avoid potential legal pitfalls. Although familiarity with relevant ethical standards is important, a discussion of these standards is presented only to the extent to which they may influence relevant legal standards. Initially, a summary of the practice of clinical supervision is presented. The purpose of this discussion is to aid the reader in forming a foundation of how clinical supervision is viewed by professionals and how the courts may also view supervision if cases related to the practice are heard.

The doctrine of *respondeat superior*, or vicarious liability, is one of the most important legal concepts in this monograph. The literal meaning of this term is *let the master respond*. It defines a supervisor's legal responsibility for the actions of the supervisee. Generally, the concept of *respondeat superior* holds that the supervisor may be liable for the damages occasioned by the negligence of the supervisee solely as a result of the supervisory relationship, thus the supervisor is vicariously liable. This type of liability will always be a potential threat to clinical supervisors.

The discussion of confidentiality and privileged communication addresses the issue of confidentiality among client, supervisee, and supervisor. Discussing clients in group meetings with others in training programs or in agency settings is considered. Additionally, record keeping, especially as it relates to confidentiality, and limits of confidentiality are reviewed.

Supervisor competence is addressed as viewed by the court. Courts generally look to standards for both training and experience in the field in determining whether a supervisor has acted competently. Specific requirements for supervisors put forth by the American Counseling Association in *Standards for Counseling Supervisors* (1989) are discussed.

Due process is a constitutional protection that is based on the 5th and 14th Amendments to the United States Constitution as well as state constitutions. A state can not deprive individuals of their rights without due process of law, which generally includes the rights to notice and a hearing where the individual's side is heard. Due process is important to supervisors in training programs where students may be terminated based on poor performance and to supervisors who are managers or employers of individuals working in a state-funded agency or hospital. Suggestions for the supervisor on how to avoid potential lawsuits by the supervisee are presented.

Dual relationships between supervisors and supervisees are viewed as problematic in all helping professions. The impropriety of having a sexual relationship with a supervisee is addressed specifically by most of the helping professions, and some extend unethical behavior to having any type of informal relationship with the supervisee. The legal aspects of this controversial issue are addressed.

Informed consent involves presenting clients and patients with information regarding the therapeutic process. Supervisees who do not provide such information to clients, especially the fact that there is a supervisor who will also be privy to information presented in counseling sessions, may be held liable for breach of confidentiality or fraud for not representing themselves as supervisees.

"Frequently Asked Questions" and "Guidelines for Practice" address specific questions and concerns and may reveal other aspects of the supervisory process not addressed earlier. The suggested readings and references provide information for readers who are interested in exploring in depth the topics covered in this monograph.

In any overview of legal issues, it must be noted that the laws and court decisions of each state may vary widely. This monograph summarizes the legal rules and standards generally followed in most states. Each clinical supervisor should, however, always determine the specific rules of law followed in his or her own state. For guidance on specific legal issues, legal counsel should be consulted.

Glossary

Case Law: Judge-made law that is generally not codified (written down or compiled) anywhere other than in the record of the case(s) in which the rule of law was pronounced by the court.

Civil Case: Every case other than a criminal proceeding. Most civil cases involve a lawsuit brought by one person against another. A civil case often involves money damages but might also have as its object the recovery of private or civil rights.

Civil Liability: The legal responsibility of a person for his or her wrong actions, or the wrong actions of another, toward another person.

Clinical Supervision: An intensive interpersonally focused one-to-one relationship in which one person is designated to promote the development of therapeutic competence in the other person.

Code: A collection or compilation of laws. For example, most states have criminal codes, and some have codes containing all laws that are related to specific subjects such as education, commercial enterprises, and mental health.

Common Law: A body of law that originates from customs and rulings of the court rather than from laws created by the legislatures.

Competence: The ability to provide adequate care or services based not only on basic knowledge and training in specific areas but also on practical abilities and skills related to the discipline.

Confidentiality: An ethical standard by which the counselor is obligated not to reveal information obtained from the client during the counseling interview to a third party without the express permission of the client.

Criminal Case: A case involving an alleged violation by an individual of specific state or federal laws. Unlike civil cases, the state is a party to the procedure and prosecutes the defendant.

Criminal Liability: The legal responsibility for the violation of any federal, state, or municipal law.

Damages: A compensation in money for a loss, injury, or deterioration of a person caused by the negligence of another.

Defendant: The person against whom a legal action is brought. This legal action may be civil or criminal.

Expert Witness: An individual who has specialized knowledge or background that could aid a judge or jury in forming a decision in a lawsuit. An expert witness must be recognized by the court in each individual case and offers opinion testimony rather than solely factual testimony.

Fiduciary: A relationship between persons in which one person acts for another in a position of trust.

Holding: The decision rendered and the rule of law on which it is based in a given court decision. This is the judge's opinion that applies the law to the facts of the case.

Informed Consent: A client's agreement to a specific treatment, therapy, and procedure based on a full disclosure and explanation by the counselor of facts needed to make an appropriate decision. In a counseling relationship, the client's informed consent should always be obtained.

Libel and Slander: Terms referring to the injury of another person's reputation. Slander is communicated by the spoken word and libel by the written word.

Licensing: A means of regulating the practice of a profession (and/or the use of a title) in which an individual proves certain competencies by examination and other requirements.

Malpractice: Harm to another individual due to negligence consisting of the breach of a professional duty or standard of care. If, for example, a mental health professional fails to follow acceptable standards for practice and harm to clients results, the professional is liable for the harm caused.

Negligence: A departure from what is acceptable as the recognized standard of practice or what is reasonable under the circumstances. Negligence implies that due care was not exercised.

Plaintiff: The one who initiates a lawsuit claiming an injury or harm due to the wrongful act of another.

Precedent: A previous court decision on a question of law that gives direction on how to decide a similar question of law in a later case with similar facts.

Privileged Communication: The legal right granted to certain professionals, such as counselors, excusing them from testifying in a court of law regarding communications between the professional and his or her clients made in the context of the professional relationship. Generally, the privilege exists for the protection of the client and in order to protect the sanctity of the professional relationship.

Respondeat Superior: A doctrine assuming that the responsibility for negligent acts of a person acting on behalf of another falls both on the actor and the person for whom he or she is acting. If a supervisee acts negligently and injures a client, then the supervisor may be held jointly liable for the injury. *Respondeat superior*, which means let the master respond, is sometimes referred to as vicarious liability.

Statutory Law: Written laws enacted by the local, state, or federal legislatures.

Subpoena Duces Tecum: An order of the court requiring that a specific person not only appear before the court for a trial or hearing but also bring specific items as described in the order and present them before the court. Penalty for noncompliance could include a jail sentence and a fine.

Tort: A civil wrong done by one person to another.

The Practice of Clinical Supervision

The very nature of supervision involves one person overseeing the behavior of another, and many believe the most essential component of supervision is the working relationship formed between these two individuals. Clinical supervision specifically involves a relationship in which supervisors possess certain qualities and experiences that allow them to aid and direct supervisees in developing similar skills and building successful experiences. Indeed, the whole process of clinical supervision is geared toward providing the supervisee with the most complete training and the necessary experience to reach professional maturity. The nature of mental health counseling, in which the counselor must attempt to identify and resolve factors often of great complexity and always of paramount importance to the emotional and psychological well-being of the client, make it essential that the counseling supervisee receive direction and supervision of the highest order. People who seek out the mental health counselor are emotionally distressed to some degree and are seeking help in personal growth or working toward emotional stability. It is unthinkable to send a mental health counselor into the real world with only academic training and no practical hands-on experience. The process of supervision provides the best scenario for enabling novice and inexperienced mental health counselors to gain the necessary skills and experience without having to rely solely on their own training, but the process is not without potential legal problems.

Clinical supervision has been discussed frequently in the literature (e.g., Borders, 1986; Burlew et al., 1992; Hart, 1982; Hess, 1980, 1987; Littrell, Lee-Borden, & Lorenz, 1979; Loganbill, Hardy, & Delworth, 1982; Stoltenberg, 1981). Topics have included the goals of supervision, models of supervision, characteristics of the supervisor and the supervisee, and the characteristics of supervision related to specific settings such as postsecondary institutions, hospitals, and agencies. In regard to models of supervision, the various roles the supervisor may play during the supervisory process have been addressed (Bernard, 1979; Hess, 1980). In general these roles include teacher, counselor, consultant, and evaluator.

Supervisors who play the teacher role are more than likely to find the supervisee lacking knowledge in various areas and thus must either provide the supervisee with that information or direct the supervisee to sources that provide that information. Supervisees in their first practicum experience are likely to require this supervisory role, especially at the beginning of the practicum. However, supervisees who have their masters or doctor of philosophy degree and are near the end of their required hours and experience for licensure may only periodically require their supervisor to be in the teacher role.

Occasionally, the supervisor must be in a counselor role during the supervisory process. The supervisee may encounter a client who brings up issues that are sensitive for the supervisee, hence causing personal discomfort to the point that the counseling process is hindered. The supervisor, recognizing the potential for harm to the client, may play the role of counselor by briefly exploring these personal issues with the supervisee. If the supervisor determines that the personal issues need to be addressed further, a request that the supervisee enter into counseling with another professional counselor is likely be made. Continuing to counsel such a supervisee constitutes an ethical violation and possible future legal problem.

Supervisors who function as consultants in the supervisory process usually are able to play this role due to the advanced development of the supervisee. As the supervisee gains knowledge and experience, the supervisor may provide alternative interventions or strategies, additional case conceptualizations, and encouragement rather than the answers required in the teacher role. Additionally, a licensed professional counselor may seek occasional supervision on cases where the counselor's experience is limited. For example, a professional counselor may encounter a client with problems of sex addiction and may have limited experience with this issue. Supervision of this counselor by a professional counselor more experienced in this area is apt to be consultative in nature.

The evaluator role in clinical supervision focuses on the performance of the supervisee. This supervisor role pervades the supervision process and should work in conjunction with the already mentioned roles throughout the supervision process (Bradley, 1989; Burlew et al., 1992; Stenack & Dye, 1982). The evaluating supervisor ascertains the effectiveness of the supervisee's counseling, identifies areas in need of improvement, gives constructive feedback, and encourages supervisee self-evaluation. Additionally, supervisors in this role provide supervisees with the criteria for successful performance and the methods used in the evaluation process. Several aspects of the evaluative role of the supervisor have legal implications and are addressed in this monograph's discussions of due process and dual relationships.

Models of supervision also include the supervisor's theory of psychotherapy (Hess, 1987). It seems that many clinical supervisors rely on their chosen theoretical orientation for counseling in the process of supervision. Those adhering to Carl Roger's theory may use the client-centered approach not only with clients but also with supervisees during supervision. However, some believe a supervisor's use of a specific theoretical base such as psychodynamic, existential, cognitive, or behavioral is relatively unimportant for effective supervision. Markowitz (1958) found that the working relationship between the supervisor and supervisee is the most critical factor for effective supervision, greater in importance than the theoretical persuasion of the supervisor.

In addition to the critical supervisory characteristics regarding roles, theoretical orientation, and the ability to form working relationships with supervisees, the literature has identified qualities of the supervisor that relate to counseling competence.

Hart (1982, p. 225) stated that "Training programs at universities and in community agencies need to insure that competent supervisors are also competent clinicians." Hart also noted that "...the point is clear that longevity of service or therapeutic expertise is not enough to qualify for a position as a supervisor, nor to fulfill effectively the duties of that position as required by the agency director and the supervisees." Thus, the effective clinical supervisor must possess both experience and good clinical skills as a counselor as well as the characteristics that allow the supervisor to foster those counseling skills in the supervisee.

Most clinicians now feel that in addition to training, experience, and expertise as a clinician, supervisors should have specialized training in the role of supervisor. Hess and Hess (1983) found that only one third of the internship sites accredited by the American Psychological Association provided training for clinical supervisors, and only 20% of training directors in such settings considered this training quite important. They also found that supervisors in their study had an average of 9.3 years of clinical experience and 7.6 years of supervisory experience, but none of these individuals had formal supervisory training. Fortunately, the present trend for training doctoral level professional counselors appears to be much different from that found by Hess and Hess among psychology clinicians.

Most counseling programs in postsecondary institutions provide course work in supervision, and this training has been addressed frequently in the literature (e.g., Bernard, 1981; Borders, 1983; Borders & Leddick, 1987; Cross & Brown, 1983; Heppner & Roehlke, 1984). The American Association of Marriage and Family Therapists (AAMFT) now recognizes a category called *approved supervisor*. A person requesting membership in this category must have experience as a supervisor and training as a supervisor of marriage and family therapists. This is evidence that AAMFT recognizes the need for specialized training and experience, beyond competence as a therapist, to be an effective supervisor.

Some states have recognized the special category of supervisor in various mental health fields and have addressed this status in their state laws. For example, South Carolina's licensing law for professional counselors, associate counselors, and marriage and family therapists states that the licensing board may not only establish criteria for qualifications for a supervisor but also may issue a license for a marital and family therapist supervisor or counselor supervisor (S.C. Code Ann., 1991). The Georgia law (Ga. Code Ann., 1991) regarding professional counselors, social workers, and marriage and family therapists states in its definitions that "supervisor means a person who meets the requirements established by the standards committee for that specialty which is being supervised and who is either licensed under this chapter or is a psychiatrist or a psychologist." Florida's mental health counselors law (Fla. Stat. Ann., 1987) states that supervision of postmasters counselor interns will be done by licensed mental health counselors, but if the intern counsels in an independent practice setting, the setting must have a licensed mental health counselor or equivalent on the premises.

The recognition of the special category of supervisor as defined by specific qualifications regarding training and experience in state law is establishing standards that are likely to become national standards, eventually. This likelihood is extremely important in relation to legal issues. As the standard develops and becomes more uniform, the courts will probably begin to evaluate the actions of supervisors in light of these accepted standards in claims of malpractice brought against supervisors.

Respondeat Superior or Vicarious Liability

Respondeat superior is a legal doctrine holding that one who occupies a position of authority or direct control over another (such as a master and servant, employer and employee, or supervisor and supervisee) can be held legally liable for the damages of another suffered as a result of the negligence of the subordinate. This doctrine is sometimes referred to as vicarious liability.

In the context of clinical supervision, the doctrine of *respondeat superior* simply means that the supervisor may be legally liable for any injury caused by the negligence of supervisees. If the supervisor is held vicariously liable and is required to pay the claimant's damages, then the supervisor, if found not to have been negligent himself or herself, may, in turn, recover those damages from the supervisee.

Generally, the supervisor may only be held liable for the negligent acts of supervisees if these acts are performed in the course and scope of the supervisory relationship. In determining whether the supervisee's alleged negligent act falls within the course and scope of the supervisory relationship, the courts will consider such factors as the following:

- the supervisor's power to control the supervisee. (For example, a supervisor who is also the employer or a university professor presumably has more power to control the supervisee than a volunteer on-site practicum or internship supervisor.)

- the supervisee's duty to perform the act. (For example, the clear duty of the supervisee is to recommend general methods for solving the client's stated problem as distinguished from the lack of any duty to advise the client to make specific decisions on, for example, divorcing or using corporal punishment.)
- the time, place, and purpose of the act. (For example, an act that occurs in the supervisee's office or during a counseling session, whether in person or by telephone, meant to further or enhance the counseling process is presumably within the course and scope of the relationship, whereas an act that occurs in a chance social meeting or in a public place and is not intended to further the counseling process probably is not.)
- the motivation of the supervisee for committing the act. (For example, an act by which the supervisee intends to produce some benefit to the client is presumably within the course and scope, whereas one in which the supervisee acts purely from his or her own personal interest and in disregard of the client's welfare, such as engaging in sexual contact with the client, likely is not.)
- whether the supervisor could have reasonably expected that the supervisee would commit the act. (For example, the supervisor can reasonably expect the supervisee to advise the sexually addictive client or the chronic alcoholic or gambler of methods available for altering the undesirable behavior, whereas he or she can not reasonably expect the occurrence of proscribed sexual contact with the client or advice to an alcoholic that he or she try marijuana instead or that a chronic gambler switch from betting on horses to investing all his or her money in stock of the XYZ Company.)

These factors are considered jointly by the court with no one factor being solely determinative of the issue. When, after considering all of the relevant factors, the court determines that the act complained of occurred within the course and scope of the supervisory relationship, then the supervisor is held vicariously liable for the harm caused by the negligence of the supervisee.

One notable circumstance in which the issue of course and scope is raised for the supervisor and in which the courts have not been uniform in deciding whether the act of the supervisee is within the course and scope of the supervisory relationship is that involving supervisees who have had sexual relations or other ethically proscribed close contact with their clients or their clients' relatives or close associates. The number of such malpractice claims against counselors seems to have rapidly increased, and it is very difficult to predict the direction in which the courts are likely to move in deciding the issue of vicarious liability in such cases. Therefore, the clinical supervisor is well advised to institute a policy of informing each supervisee, preferably in writing, of the ethical and legal proscriptions against such contact, with the reasons for this proscription, and obtain a signed acknowledgment that the supervisee has been so informed.

Most acts that might be performed by the supervisee and cause injury to the client, or a third party having some relationship to the client, are likely to be deemed to have been committed within the course and scope of the supervisory relationship, thus leading to the supervisor's vicarious liability. The supervisor's focus, therefore, should be on strategies designed to eliminate the likelihood that a supervisee will perform negligently. These strategies are discussed throughout this work in detail and include taking an active role in the initial screening and assessing of the supervisee's competence, selecting specific client treatment plans, facilitating the treatment, continuing involvement in the ongoing treatment, and adherence to a standard clinical procedure for case review (Vesper & Brock, 1991).

One of the most difficult decisions for the supervisor is the determination of how often and in what form specific case review with the supervisee should occur, that is, how much control the supervisor should assume over the supervisee. This is also a perplexing problem for the attorney advising the supervisor because there are conflicting notions about what course of action places the supervisor on the firmest legal ground.

Simply stated, the controversy among attorneys is whether it is wiser for the supervisor to assume more or less of the available control over the supervisee. This controversy stems from disagreement among attorneys as to which standard a court is likely to apply in judging a supervisor's conduct. Traditionally, any professional whose conduct is called into question in a negligence action is held to have a duty to act according to the generally accepted practices within the profession. Any conduct that is deemed to have fallen below that standard is considered negligent conduct. Given such a rule, many attorneys advise that minimal control, or that which just rises to the level of the generally accepted practices within the profession, is wisest. This course of action assumes that the supervisor's actual control of the supervisee is a primary factor in determining the supervisor's liability for his or her own negligence, that is, the less actual control assumed, the less likelihood of a finding of negligent supervision. Thus it is reasoned that the supervisor should only seek to assume enough control to meet the minimal standard of the generally accepted practices within the profession, thereby minimizing the probability of a court finding that the supervisor was in control of the supervisee's negligent act. According to this rationale, it might be advisable that the supervisor only meet regularly, such as once a week, to review problem cases with the supervisee and only maintain minimal direct knowledge or control of other cases handled by the supervisee.

However, this line of reasoning, although perhaps having some merit regarding avoidance of the supervisor's own negligence, has little value as a strategy against a finding of vicarious liability. This is true because the courts, when considering the issue of whether the complained of act is within the course and scope of the supervisory relationship, consider how much control is reasonably available to the supervisor rather than how much actual control is assumed.

Another view is that of those attorneys who argue that as communication and the dissemination of information increase within any profession, the courts will seek more and more to hold professionals to a duty to perform according to ideal ethical standards, such as the guidelines adopted by the Association for Counselor Education and Supervision (ACES) in 1993 (see appendix A), because such standards constitute what are or should be the practices generally accepted within the profession. These attorneys argue that the supervisor should seek to control the supervisee in conformity with the highest ethical standards adopted by the professional association in order to avoid any negligent conduct and to insure the greatest probability of competent supervisee performance. This line of reasoning assumes that the courts are likely to give more weight to the level of control available to the supervisor than to the actual amount of control assumed by the supervisor and to find the supervisor directly negligent for not assuming enough control. Based on this rationale, the attorney's recommendation might be to review tapes of every counseling session conducted by the supervisee.

The difficult problem of advising the supervisor as to how much case review is enough rests, in the final analysis, on trying to balance the circumstances that are most likely to lead to the supervisor's direct negligence against the circumstances that are most likely to lead to vicarious liability for the supervisee's negligence. It is recommended here that the supervisor err on the side of assuming more, rather than less, control in the area of case review. Further, it is recommended that the supervisor act in accordance with all applicable sections of the 1993 ACES *Ethical Guidelines for Counseling Supervisors* on this issue. In commenting on this problem and reaching a similar conclusion, Woody (1985) stated that

> Conformity to applicable standards of care requires knowledge of those standards. Most professional organizations in the mental health field have both codes of ethics and written guidelines for the delivery of professional services.... If clinicians do nothing else to protect themselves from malpractice claims, they should become familiar with such publications and conform their practices to the standards dictated therein. (p. 521)

It is sometimes difficult for even the attorney to maintain clearly the distinction between the liability of the supervisor for his or her own negligence in the performance of the supervisory role and the vicarious liability of the supervisor for the supervisee's negligence. The two often seem to overlap, as in the factors regarding control. For example, a client who alleges that injury occurred due to treatment or counseling received from a supervisee might claim several possible alternative theories of negligence. The supervisee could have administered the treatment negligently in spite of proper supervision. The supervisor could have been negligent in advising the supervisee as to proper treatment method and technique or in failing to maintain adequate involvement in the counseling process, thus allowing the supervisee to counsel outside his or her sphere of competence. The supervisor could have been negligent in initially screening and assessing the supervisee's competence as a candidate and in admitting the supervisee into the clinical program.

With regard to claims of the supervisor's own negligence, the courts are more likely to find the supervisor directly negligent when it is shown that the supervisor failed to be actively involved in and aware of the treatment process, and less likely to find the supervisor directly negligent when the supervisor was active involved in the treatment process but made an error in judgment (Wilkinson, 1982). This tendency makes it particularly important to develop a well-defined clinical procedure for case review and to document adherence to the procedure for evidence in presenting a defense to claims of the supervisor's own negligence. Vesper and Brock (1991) have offered a model for developing a sound clinical procedure that consists of

1. a clearly defined outline of the frequency with which supervision must occur (e.g., weekly, bimonthly);
2. a method of identifying client problems;
3. careful delineation of the treatment plan;
4. description of how to implement the treatment plan; and
5. discussion of desired and expected outcomes, as well as probable pitfalls in accomplishing the treatment plan. (p. 67)

Following such a clinical procedure is also critical in instances involving the supervisor's vicarious liability. If the supervisor is held vicariously liable for the damages suffered by a client injured as the result of a supervisee's negligence, the supervisor might be able to recover from the supervisee what the supervisor is required to pay. In order to do so, however, the supervisor must be able to show documented evidence that the supervisor was not directly negligent in any way. This can be done by showing strict adherence to the procedure for case review and other supervisory procedures, which is much more likely when the type of clinical procedure just outlined is followed.

In summary, the issue of *respondeat superior*, or vicarious liability, is potentially one of the most important legal principles for clinical supervisors. Even the most competent supervisor who performs the role flawlessly can still be liable for the actions of supervisees. It can be said that those who supervise must be even more diligent in the role of supervisor than in the role of counselor in order to limit the potentially disastrous effect of a claim of vicarious liability. The diligent supervisor should determine and conform to the applicable standards of care within the counseling profession, communicate those standards to supervisees and (directly or indirectly) to the supervisee's clients, review the conduct of the supervisee on a regular basis to determine that the conduct is competent and according to the applicable standards of care, and document all aspects of the supervisory and counseling procedures whenever possible.

Confidentiality and Privileged Communication

One of the most essential qualities of good counseling practice is confidentiality. The client relies on confidentiality, and this confidentiality fosters the full and honest communication necessary for effective counseling. Both ethically and legally any breach of this confidentiality tends to undermine the counseling process. Therefore, our legal system has come to include both statutes and common law precedents that recognize the confidential relationship between a counselor and client. As a threshold consideration, note that confidential communications include not only information communicated directly by the client to the counselor, either orally or in writing, but also client records and such "client materials" as video- or audiotapes, test results, charts, and notes.

The issue of confidentiality can arise in two different contexts for the counselor. The first is that the counselor owes a duty of confidentiality to the client. Should the counselor breach that duty, he or she might be subject to a civil action for malpractice brought by the client. The second context is that the counselor might be ordered to appear before a court for the purpose of giving testimony on some issue that involves the client in either a civil or criminal matter and that requires the counselor to reveal confidential information before the court. These two circumstances are considered separately.

A claim for damages brought by the client against the counselor for breach of confidentiality virtually always is based on alleged malpractice as a theory of negligence. In order for a client to recover damages due to the negligence of the counselor (i.e., malpractice), the client must prove that the counselor owed a duty to the client, that the counselor breached the duty, and that the breach of the duty caused the client's injuries.

Although there are many factors that define, in a particular circumstance, whether or not a duty of confidentiality is owed by the counselor to the client, here only those issues of confidentiality specifically relevant to the supervisor are discussed. For guidance in determining under which circumstances the duty exists for the counselor, it is advisable to consult the applicable state laws as well as relevant ethical canons and guidelines. Generally, however, the duty exists when the communication is made in confidence, and it is understood that the client desires that the communication remain confidential.

One factor relevant in determining whether a duty of confidentiality exists and particularly important in the context of clinical supervision is whether the communication is made in the presence of a third party. The courts in general have held that a communication made in the presence of a third party, where there is some confidential relationship involving that party, is a confidential communication. Certainly the relationship that exists between the supervisor and supervisee is such that communications by the client in the presence of the supervisor are confidential. Further, it must be remembered that any confidential communication made to the supervisor, whether directly by the client or by the supervisee at a later time, imposes the duty of confidentiality on the supervisor.

A related issue, which arises in the context of clinical supervision, is that of informing the client of the supervisory relationship and obtaining the client's consent to share confidential communications with the supervisor. Failure to disclose this relationship fully and obtain the necessary consent could subject both the supervisor and supervisee to a claim of negligent breach of confidentiality.

The supervisor, in order to avoid the possibility of such a claim, should fully review with the supervisee the general ethical duty of confidentiality owed to the client with specific reference to the applicable laws and relevant ethical standards. Additionally, steps must be taken to see that the client is fully advised of both the nature of confidentiality (i.e., the rights of the client and the duties of the supervisee) and of the existence of the supervisory relationship, and that the client's consent to participate and share confidential communications with the supervisor is secured, preferably in writing. The supervisor must also preside over the strict adherence to the ethical duty of confidentiality by the supervisee through the procedure for case review discussed in the section on *respondeat superior*.

Bernard and O'Laughlin (1990) identified seven elements necessary for establishing a clinic policy to assure confidentiality. Those seven elements can be summarized as follows:

1. Ethical standards and canons regarding confidentiality must be identified and discussed with supervisees.
2. Confidentiality of client materials must be maintained.
3. Security of client materials must be maintained.
4. Prohibition of nonprofessional discussion must be insured.
5. Prohibition of disclosure of client identity must be insured.
6. Clients must be informed of clinic policies regarding confidentiality and ethics.
7. Exceptions to confidentiality and privileged communications must be identified and discussed with supervisees and clients.

It is strongly suggested that the clinical supervisor refer to these seven elements in adopting a clinic policy to insure the supervisee's compliance with the duty of confidentiality .

The second context in which the issue of confidentiality arises for the supervisor is when he or she is ordered to appear before a court for the purpose of giving testimony regarding the client. This circumstance may arise in either a civil or criminal matter.

The issue of confidentiality as applied to the testimony in court of the counselor or supervisor is referred to in legal terms as *privileged communication*. Generally, for the purpose of fostering trust in the counseling relationship, most confidential communications between a counselor and client are considered privileged, that is, the counselor can not be forced to breach the confidentiality by revealing the substance of these communications in open court. Any communication made to the supervisor, whether by the client or supervisee, is also considered privileged. However, although all privileged communications are confidential communications, some confidential communications may not be privileged, and the courts generally require some statutory authority as a basis for finding a particular communication to be privileged. Furthermore, there are statutes in many states that define particular exceptions to otherwise privileged communications, such as the obligation of a counselor to testify in a child custody hearing. The supervisor should identify and become familiar with applicable state statutes regarding privileged statements as they define the duty to testify in given circumstances. If the supervisor has any doubts as to his or her duty to testify in a given situation, legal counsel is advised.

This statutory basis for finding a statement to be privileged is one factor distinguishing privileged communications (those which the witness is not required to divulge when subpoenaed to testify) and confidential communications (those which the supervisor is ethically, and thereby legally, bound to keep confidential or risk a claim of negligent breach of confidentiality by the client). The basis for determining whether a particular statement is confidential is generally the applicable ethical standards and guidelines of the profession.

Based on the same rationale discussed in relation to negligent breach of confidentiality, it is reasonable to believe that the courts will extend any statutory authority granting privileged communications to counselors to include supervisors. Therefore, as a practical matter, the supervisor should be familiar with some general principles of the law of privileged communication—which will help them understand the rights and obligations of the individual called as a witness. Central to this understanding is the notion that the privilege exists for the benefit of the client, not for the supervisor. Thus, the privilege can be waived by the client, in which case the witness is obligated to testify fully.

In addition, the privilege does not apply in those circumstances specifically excepted by statute and in which the witness is compelled to provide otherwise confidential information to the court. These circumstances may vary slightly from state to state, but generally they are uniform. Corey, Corey, and Callanan (1993) discussed these circumstances, which can be summarized as follows:

1. when the therapist is appointed by the court;
2. when there is a suicide risk;
3. when a malpractice suit is initiated against the therapist;
4. when a client's mental health is questioned as part of a civil action;
5. when a child is a victim of a crime;
6. when the client is a danger to self or others;
7. when the client needs hospitalization; or
8. if the client expresses the intent to commit a crime that will endanger society or another person.

Thus if a statutory privileged communication exists, the supervisor is not compelled by law to reveal any confidential information before a court except when the client waives the privilege or when an exception such as those just listed exists. Each counselor and supervisor must be fully aware of these obligations and be able to determine the duty to testify depending on the particular situation at hand. Failure to do so may lead to a claim for damages due to breach of confidentiality when testimony is not legally mandated, or to civil liability and/or criminal sanctions due to refusing to testify when testimony is mandated. Legal consultation is advised when confidential information is demanded.

One specific area of the law involving confidentiality that is constantly developing and holds the potential for liability for the supervisor concerns the issue of the duty to protect third parties from a dangerous client as first pronounced in the seminal case of *Tarasoff v. Regents of the University of California* (1976). A good discussion of the *Tarasoff* principle and its subsequent development by the courts is found in Felthous (1989). A particular point of concern for the supervisor is the rule, developed from *Tarasoff,* that the supervisor's ignorance of a circumstance involving an issue of confidentiality that eventually leads to the injury of another (including the client) might not be a defense to the failure to protect. Presumably, the issue of the supervisor's ability to control the supervisee could be a crucial factor, and the same issues discussed regarding vicarious liability could determine the supervisor's best course of action in preventing liability. It is suggested that the supervisor actively participate in the clinical procedure for case review, maintain a diligent effort to remain abreast of all matters involving confidentiality, and take an active role in determining when the duty to protect requires that confidentiality be breached.

Finally, it is suggested that the supervisor be responsible for the continuing education of both the supervisor and supervisee as to the legal duties and obligations involving confidentiality—which are in a constant state of flux. It is recommended that at least one member of the clinic's supervisory staff annually attend a legal seminar dealing specifically with issues of confidentiality and privileged communication and then present these issues to the entire staff.

Competence

Competence as a clinical supervisor is important in the supervisory process. It is also essential if legal action is brought against the supervisor. Those in the helping professions view competence as the ability to provide adequate care and services and as based on both knowledge in specific areas and practical abilities and skills related to the discipline. *Black's Law Dictionary* (1990) in defining competence used such phrases as "duly qualified," "answering all requirements," and "having sufficient ability, capacity, or authority." This dictionary described one who is duly qualified as one who possesses every qualification generally recognized essential in a particular discipline and who has achieved a particular professional status based on achievement in the field.

The issues of training and practice of supervision have been addressed elsewhere in the professional literature (Cormier & Bernard, 1982; Hess, 1987; Stoltenberg & Delworth, 1987). Stoltenberg and Delworth recognized the importance of training in clinical supervision as a factor of competence and stated that "just as we now consider it unethical to counsel without prior training we may soon apply the same idea to supervision" (p. 171).

Principle A of the American Psychological Association (APA) *Ethical Principles of Psychologists and Code of Conduct* (1992) is the only principle that seems related to clinical supervisor competence in the practice of psychology. This principle emphasizes the necessity for high standards of competence for all psychologists and addresses the importance of psychologists only providing services for which they are qualified by education, training, or experience. Does this principle suggest that a psychologist have some formal training in clinical supervision in order to qualify as a competent supervisor?

Even though this issue of competence for psychologists who supervise was addressed in the early 1980s (Newman, 1981), no formal set of guidelines for psychologist supervisors has been developed. Newman, however, presented some interesting questions regarding supervisor competence:

1. Has the supervisor had training in the theory and practice of supervision or in the supervised practice of psychotherapy supervision?
2. Do the supervisors conscientiously practice the skills they are helping their trainees learn?
3. Has the supervisor had training or experience in the assessment or treatment of the types of clinical problems and clients seen by the trainee?
4. If the supervisor is not adequately qualified, has supervision by a qualified clinician been arranged or has the trainee's client been referred elsewhere? (p. 292)

Even though other mental health professions have addressed the need for high standards of competence and most have adopted standards, the Association for Counselor Education and Supervision remains the only mental health group that has a set of published standards designed especially for counseling supervisors (see appendix B). The ACES *Standards for Counseling Supervisors* (1989) set forth important characteristics of competent and effective supervisors, including personal traits, knowledge, and practical abilities. The court is likely to consider the actual *practice* of supervision rather than ideal standards in determining supervisor competence when it is a relevant consideration in a particular case at hand, but the court may refer to these standards as a guide.

The ACES standards are based on 11 core areas related to personal traits, knowledge, and competencies of effective supervisors. In addition, the education and training of supervisors is delineated. The first core area states that professional counseling supervisors must be effective counselors who have both knowledge and skills gained through training and supervised employment. Thus consideration for the courts to determine the competence of a supervisor could be a consideration of the supervisor's graduate training and effectiveness in counseling.

The second core area addresses a supervisor's personal traits and characteristics. These include possessing a sense of humor, being optimistic, being comfortable in the role of supervisor, and being able to encourage and motivate the supervisee. Clearly, these traits are subjective and idealistic and nearly impossible for the courts to assess. However, another part of this core area, the requirement that counseling supervisors update their counseling and supervisory skills, involves continuing education activities that are much more easily documented.

The remaining core areas require that the supervisor demonstrate knowledge in several areas. These include knowledge of ethical, legal, and regulatory aspects of the profession; the personal and professional nature of the supervisory relationship; supervision methods and techniques; counselor developmental process; case conceptualization and management; assessment and evaluation; oral and written reporting and recording; evaluation of counseling performance; and research in counseling and counseling supervision. Knowledge in all these areas can be achieved by formal preparation or training, and competence can be established through practice as a supervisor.

In addition to these 11 core areas related to competency in counseling supervision, preparation for this role is specifically addressed. The counseling supervisor needs not only graduate training in counseling but also graduate training in counseling supervision. The basic curriculum should include seminars, didactic courses, laboratory courses, and supervision practica. Successful supervised employment as a professional counselor is also necessary, as are credentials in professional areas such as a state department of education or a national certification agency, or licensure as a professional counselor.

As stated, the courts in each state will look at the prevailing standards of the profession in the determination of supervisor competence. At the present time the ACES *Standards for Counseling Supervisors* (1989) represent the ideal, but in the effort toward professionalism, requiring clinical supervisors to possess the traits just summarized seems to be the trend. For example, those individuals who are licensed as counselors may not necessarily be viewed in some states as competent supervisors without additional specialty credentials. Several states have already established guidelines in their licensing laws for status as a clinical supervisor. South Carolina has a separate supervision license, and the Louisiana Licensed Professional Counselors Board of Examiners has established a set of criteria that a licensed counselor must meet in order to supervise individuals who are counselor interns seeking licensure. The courts will rely upon the standards established within the profession in each state and judge a supervisor's competence using the same distinctions between licensed professional counselors and clinical supervisors as those made by the state's professional groups. Present or prospective clinical supervisors are urged to examine the existing licensure laws in their own state for guidance.

In addition to specialty training and experience, an objective assessment instrument to evaluate supervisory competence may be used by counselor supervisors to assess their skills. These results may be important if the supervisor's competence is challenged in court. These instruments, several of which were presented by Stoltenberg and Delworth (1987), measure many clinical supervisor characteristics, including the evidence of supervisor roles and behavior, time spent in various supervisory functions, affective focus of supervision, cognitive and skills focus of supervision, approach to a theoretical framework, and supervisor impact on various counseling skills for the trainee.

As suits against those in the helping professions increase, accountability will become more important. Clinical supervisors' most effective strategies for avoiding and defeating legal challenges to their professional competence are twofold. First, the clinical supervisor should become and remain familiar with the generally recognized standards within the profession defining professional competence as a clinical supervisor and comply with those standards. Second, the clinical supervisor is advised to document compliance in all cases if possible. In the end, adherence to these two strategies may well determine whether the clinical supervisor can present an effective, successful defense to a legal challenge to professional competence.

Due Process

The due process clause of the 14th Amendment to the United States Constitution states, in pertinent part, that no state shall "deprive any person of life, liberty, or property without due process of law." This clause protects persons from state actions without first allowing that person the opportunity to oppose the proposed action. It prohibits states and educational institutions from administering unrealistically hard corporal punishment, which relates to substantive due process, and from expelling a student without allowing the student to have a hearing, which is procedural due process. The rights protected by procedural due process are more pertinent to this discussion. Procedural due process essentially provides that notice and a hearing must be given before an important right, such as the right to an education, can be removed even on a temporary basis. A key point in understanding the relevance of due process to clinical supervision is that due process protects individuals from state action, or from an individual acting on behalf of the state, but not from the actions of purely private agencies, institutions, or persons. Due process related to clinical supervision in both public and private agencies is addressed here.

Because many clinical supervisors work in state and/or federally funded postsecondary institutions, supervising practicum students and students in intern programs, knowledge of due process is extremely important as the time may come when certain students may need to be terminated from the graduate program. In postsecondary programs, supervisees should be provided with information as to the nature of the supervisory relationship just as clients are provided with information about the nature of the counseling relationship in informed consent procedures. It is at the discretion of the supervisor as to whether this information should be provided orally or in writing. Even though written consent is recommended but not legally required, understanding and acceptance of this information by supervisees is essential. Cormier and Bernard (1982) stated that supervisees in training programs have a right to know what their roles are, the expectations of the supervisor, goals that should be met, and how the supervisee is to be evaluated. Cormier and Bernard stressed the importance of providing this information to the supervisee in writing at the beginning of the supervisory process so the supervisee will know what to do to be successful in a course. A student who has been unsuccessful in completing a practicum course may bring suit against the supervisor based on the supervisor's failure to provide the student with information regarding roles and what the student needs to do to be successful. Such a supervisor may be violating the student's due process right to "notice." Further, if the supervisee can prove that dismissal from a graduate program occurred without opportunity for a hearing, a successful due process claim might be raised (Jennings, 1981; Kapp, 1981).

Several cases related to due process in academic settings are worthy of mention in this discussion. One is the 1961 case of *Dixon v. Alabama State Board of Education*. Although it was a disciplinary dismissal decision, certain elements are important. This case involved students who were dismissed from a secondary public school for cheating, stealing, drug abuse, and other violations of institutional standards of conduct. The court ruled that the students could not be dismissed without due process of law. The basic rights of due process set forth in *Dixon* are that students should receive notice, a hearing, and an explanation before being suspended or expelled from a public school (Miles, 1987). This court distinguished due process cases that involve disciplinary issues (i.e., it is a fact that the student broke a disciplinary standard) from those involving academic issues and ruled that the protection of due process rights depends on unique circumstances that must be evaluated on an individual case basis.

Another case involving a disciplinary decision that also had important effects on later academic due process cases was *Goss v. Lopez* (1975). The court in this case ruled that if a student can prove that an academic termination has harmed or will harm his or her good name, reputation, honor, or integrity and was done without opportunity to clear that harm, a graduate faculty or institution could be held accountable (Knoff & Prout, 1985).

Most courts are reluctant to reverse academic dismissal decisions made by qualified faculty members teaching in specialized programs. Knoff and Prout (1985) stated that

> these professional decisions or rights include the establishment of criteria or standards for student admission, course completion, remediation (if necessary), and graduation; the specification of required coursework and curricular content and format; and the determination of appropriate faculty to teach specific coursework. (p. 791)

The case of *Connelly v. University of Vermont and State Agricultural College* (1965), which involved a third-year medical student who was denied the opportunity to repeat his third year, is illustrative. The student had been ill, was allowed to make up his work missed through the summer months, but failed the summer courses. The student filed suit saying the professor had failed him arbitrarily and that the professor was prejudiced against him. Connelly was required by the court to prove his allegations, and eventually the university's decision for dismissal was upheld.

Academic due process was further defined by the courts in two other cases. In *Gaspar v. Bruton* (1975) the court held that to satisfy due process school authorities need only make students aware of their failure or impending failure to meet minimum standards prior to termination. In *Greenhill v. Bailey* (1975), a medical school dismissed Greenhill due to poor intellectual ability or lack of preparation. This case involved liberty interests, and the court ordered the medical school to allow Greenhill to respond to the stigmatizing statements. Even though the school was not required to readmit Greenhill, the court stated that Greenhill should have been informed in writing of the alleged deficiency in his intellectual ability.

Another case directly related to the counseling profession involving academic dismissal is *Shuffer v. Trustees of California State University and Colleges* (1977). Shuffer was a master's level student in the Department of Guidance and Counseling, which was part of the School of Education. Because of Shuffer's unsatisfactory performance in the required practicum, he was required to take a second, remedial practicum. The court ruled that the faculty may fashion special requirements for students who are deficient in certain areas. However, these requirements can be neither arbitrary nor impulsive but must be based on the university's familiarity with the student involved and the judgment of the professors who are responsible for preparing the student for professional life.

These cases emphasize how the courts view training program faculty and procedures as well as student rights regarding termination. The courts appear to support faculty autonomy in establishing academic and experiential procedures, but the faculty are expected to provide these procedures. In order to satisfy this expectation of the court, a formal policy regarding both personal and professional development and academic and skill-related growth should be provided to all supervisees in an academic setting at the onset of a practicum course or an internship. Even though few suits against educators based on violation of due process rights, including suits brought against counselor supervisors by student counselors, have been successful, those who educate and train student counselors in postsecondary programs should not become complacent. McAfee and Cote (1985) have aptly stated that in our litigious society "the issue of professional liability for educators and trainers is a bomb waiting to explode" (p. 56).

The constitutional due process requirement is limited to public institutions or those which receive significant state or federal funds. Private institutions are not required to provide due process unless the requirement is written into their own handbooks or formal policy statements. In *VanLook v. Curran* (1986) the Alabama Supreme Court held that if a private school's contract with the parents or student includes provisions for due process, the private school must grant the students due process. In this case the school had made a choice to include due process in the contract even though the school was not required to do so (Miles, 1987).

The same is true of private agencies and private hospitals. A supervisee who works in a private agency or hospital that has a due process clause in the employee contract may bring suit against a supervisor if the supervisor failed to provide the supervisee with detailed information regarding successful employment and the supervisee was terminated. Mental health practitioners who supervise other mental health workers are advised to provide specific information regarding supervisees' performance for satisfactory employment. When these precautions are taken, the supervisor is on much more solid ground in defending against legal action.

Requirements for supervisees in the workplace differ from requirements of supervisees in training sites. Employed supervisors are not only judged based on clinical skills but also on how well they manage their time. Robiner, Fuhrman, and Bobbitt (1990) stated that those individuals who work in a health maintenance organization or preferred provider organization may be pressed to become very efficient, especially in areas where competition in the marketplace threatens these organizations.

Number of hours of patient contact and number of patients served may be as important as actual quality of clinical work or clinical skills in an agency or hospital setting. Therefore, it is understandable that supervisees working in these settings need to be fully informed as to the expectations of their supervisors. In addition to information regarding client load, criteria to be met in order to advance in that organization or agency should also be communicated to the supervisee. Supervisors in these settings are advised to provide supervisees with this information because novice employees may have difficulty handling the case load and thus succeeding at their jobs.

Many supervisors may resist adopting a specific standard of evaluating supervisees because of the subjective nature of the process. Supervisors may also fear that too much criticism of their supervisees may jeopardize the supervisees' livelihood. This issue is addressed in the APA *Ethical Principles of Psychologists and Code of Conduct* (1992). Referring to the provisions of Principle 3, Robiner, Fuhrman, and Bobbitt (1990) suggested that an objective instrument—the Minnesota Supervisory Inventory (MSI)—be used for evaluating interns in psychology in order to insure compliance with due process standards. The MSI instrument "is intended as a comprehensive inventory addressing diverse dimensions associated with the professional practice of psychology" (p. 95).

Due process requirements dictate that supervisors strictly protect the supervisees' due process rights at every step of the supervisory process. Suggestions for doing so have been outlined and discussed. The failure of the supervisor to protect these rights can result in civil actions against the supervisor for malpractice.

Dual Relationships

When counselors blend their professional relationship with clients with other kinds of relationships, they are violating ethical standards and are skating on thin ice in a legal sense. Mental health professionals engaging in sexual relationships with their clients seem to be a popular media topic, and many of these professionals have been sued for malpractice by clients or former clients. Of the complaints filed with licensing boards of licensed professional counselors, 20% were due to sexual relationships with clients (Neukrug, Healy, & Herlihy, 1992). This category was surpassed only by practicing without a license or other misrepresentation (26%). The increase in suits brought against mental health professionals who have engaged in sexual relationships with their clients has not only added to the increase in malpractice insurance rates, but it has also led to disclaimer statements limiting or disallowing coverage for sexual misconduct in most malpractice insurance policies.

The nature of supervision places the clinical supervisor in a similar position of liability because certain kinds of dual relationships with supervisees may be difficult to avoid. Three types of dual relationships involving clinical supervisors and supervisees are sexual contact, personal counseling of the supervisee by the supervisor, and social relationships. Each of these dual relationships has inherent problems and could lead to malpractice suits or sexual harassment charges being brought against the supervisor.

Even though there is not an abundance of published information related to the first type of dual relationship, sexual relationships between supervisors and supervisees, existing research has indicated it may be a relatively common practice. A survey of psychology training programs in the United States conducted in 1979 (Pope, Levenson, & Schover, 1979) found that 10% of the students reported having had sexual contact with an instructor. Of this group, 47% of the females and 86% of the males reported having had sexual contact with a clinical supervisor. Glaser and Thorpe (1986) conducted an anonymous survey of women who were members of Division 12 of the American Psychological Association. Their questions addressed three areas:

1. the type of experience (either sexual intercourse or direct genital stimulation) with psychology educators during their graduate training and how the contact was viewed both then and currently;
2. experiences of sexual advances from educators that did not lead to sexual contact and the respondents' perceptions of these; and,
3. irrespective of their actual experiences, the respondents' opinions about the likelihood of coercion and ethicality of sexual contact between graduate students and psychology educators during a working relationship.

The results of the survey indicated that at the time of contact those engaging in this behavior viewed it neutrally. However, sexual advances were reported by 31% of the respondents, and these advances were *currently* seen by the majority as overwhelmingly negative and highly unethical.

Counselor supervisors experience dual relationship problems that may be viewed as sexual in nature, especially if they fulfill the role of mentor for some of their more eager and responsive supervisees (Bartell & Rubin, 1990). The supervisor may engage in what seems to be innocent discussions with a motivated counselor intern, practicum student, or student intern but may inadvertently develop intimate feelings neither originally desired nor expected. Instructors in the helping professions who teach clinical skills assume several roles in the supervisory process (Hess, 1980; Littrell, Lee-Borden, & Lorenz, 1979). One of these roles is evaluator, and it should be fulfilled in a highly responsible manner without sexual innuendos. The supervisor's professional judgment and objective evaluation of supervisee performance is hindered if a deeply personal intimacy, which is romantic in nature, evolves. If the supervisor begins to develop these romantic feelings toward a supervisee, another supervisor should be sought.

Another example of highly unethical conduct is when supervisors expect sexual activity for favorable supervisee evaluations or trade positive evaluations for sexual favors. Pope, Schover, and Levenson (1980) stated that "both the romantic involvement and the business exchange aspects raise serious doubts about what is being evaluated and on what basis" (p. 159). Not only does a relationship that is sexual in nature distort clear professional judgment, but also the supervisor will find it difficult to maintain objectivity in the evaluation of the supervisee. It is questionable as to whether the supervisor truly has the best interest of the supervisee in mind if sexually involved with the supervisee.

Supervisees will always be in the least powerful position in the supervisor/supervisee relationship. If this relationship becomes exploitative, the supervisee may have grounds for legal action against the supervisor. One case, though related to the client-counselor relationship, gives some interesting insight into how the court may view sexual impropriety. In *Zipkin v. Freeman* (1969), the court held that not only sexual intercourse but also lesser forms of intimate contact such as holding hands, swimming together, or attending parties could constitute malpractice by a psychotherapist in a psychotherapeutic relationship. Therefore, supervisors are well advised to be continually mindful of their behavior. Even when the supervisor acts in what may be thought of as an acceptable manner with the supervisee, the supervisee and others may view the behavior as sexual in nature.

The second type of dual relationship between supervisors and supervisees that is potentially troublesome, if not unethical and legally questionable, is when the clinical supervisor serves as the supervisee's counselor. Certain types of training programs stress analytical skills and even require their students to engage in counseling as part of their degree program. Instructors and supervisors in these specialized programs believe strongly that transference is an inevitable and desirable aspect of the supervisory relationship. However, most feel this process is questionable in the development of new skills necessary for the trainee to become an independent therapist. The general feeling is that the supervisor should not enter into a formal therapeutic relationship with a supervisee. If this type of dual relationship occurs, some aspects of the roles that the supervisor and supervisee play will conflict. For example, if a supervisor is given personal information concerning sexual abuse while the supervisee is in the client role, the supervisor may place fewer demands on the supervisee when the supervisee is working with clients who have also experienced sexual abuse. In this example the supervisor is clearly not operating in the best interest of the supervisee's client, which should be the most essential ingredient in supervision. In addition, the supervisor has lost objectivity and has failed to provide the highest standard of supervision.

The third type of problematic dual relationship is a social relationship between supervisor and supervisee. Should a supervisor supervise a trainee who also happens to be the supervisor's friend? Should a supervisor attend social events where supervisees may be present? Should a student supervisor in a doctoral level program supervise a friend who is in the practicum of a master's level program? If the supervisor wishes to avoid potential legal problems, the answer to these three questions is "No, if at all possible." Social relationships may be misconstrued or develop into what the courts may see as intimate relationships. The roles that supervisors engage in should not include friendships with the supervisees. Not only will the supervisor have problems with being objective in evaluating the supervisee, but also the friendship will be strained if the outcome of the supervisory process is less than the supervisee expected.

The inherent role of the supervisee is one of lesser power and status than that of the supervisor. The problems with dual relationships between supervisor and supervisee include diminished consent, exploitation by the supervisor, role conflict of both, reduction of the supervisor's power in some aspects of supervision, and poor objectivity on the part of the supervisor, which interferes with the ability to supervise the novice counselor adequately (Cormier & Bernard, 1982). At the present time, most of the helping professions have ethical standards regarding dual relationship behaviors in the context of supervision. The AAMFT *Code of Ethical Principles for Marriage and Family Therapists* (1988) states in Principle 4 that marriage and family therapists recognize they are potentially influential with respect to students, employees, and supervisees and avoid exploiting the trust and dependency of these individuals. Examples of dual relationships are specifically cited and include the provision of therapy to students, employees, and supervisees as well as business or close personal relationships with students, employees, or supervisees. Sexual intimacy with students or supervisees is prohibited.

In 1977, the Board of Medical Quality Assurance of the State of California, which governs the licensing of psychologists, established regulations for those who supervise and evaluate applicants for a license to practice psychology. Among the regulations is the following:

> Any experience obtained while under the supervision of a practitioner with whom the applicant has an interpersonal or familial relationship which undermines the authority of the supervisor or the effectiveness of that supervision, shall not be counted toward the hours of supervised professional experience. (Chapter 13.1, Section 1387, p. 157)

Additionally, in 1993 the Association for Counselor Education and Supervision adopted the *Ethical Guidelines for Counseling Supervisors* (see appendix A). Guideline 2.11 states that supervisors should not participate in any form of sexual contact with supervisees and that supervisors should not engage in any form of social contact or interaction that could compromise the supervisor-supervisee relationship. Additionally, Guideline 2.12 states that supervisors should not establish a psychotherapy relationship as a substitute for the supervisee's supervision. Personal issues should be addressed in supervision only in terms of the impact of these issues on clients and on professional functioning. Because the court is consistently looking to standards of treatment in their decision-making process regarding cases brought against mental health professionals, these standards and regulations could be considered in decisions regarding suits related to dual relationships brought against supervisors. Supervisors are advised to adhere to published standards and regulations in their field in respect to dual relationships in order to avoid any type of legal liability.

Informed Consent

The doctrine of informed consent was developed to require physicians to explain to patients procedures that could be potentially harmful to the patient. Physicians are required to tell patients about any problems that might develop from treatment, and this information enables patients to make intelligent decisions as to whether they want to proceed with the proposed treatment. The failure of physicians to inform patients fully constitutes malpractice and subjects physicians to potential liability for any injuries occurring as a result of the treatment. This doctrine has been extended to include other health service providers, including mental health practitioners.

States and local jurisdictions differ in their interpretation and application of informed consent standards, but there is general agreement, based on legislation and case law, on what constitutes valid consent by clients. In general, four elements must be present for informed consent to be valid (Stromberg et al., 1988). These include competency of the client, understanding by the client, disclosure of material information, and voluntary consent.

Competency, the first element of valid informed consent, relates to the ability to think rationally, and this is essential for clients to be able to make good decisions that affect them personally. When a supervisee or mental health professional works with individuals who may be retarded or emotionally disabled, competency of that client may be in question. Consent for counseling from a client who is not competent could be challenged in court as invalid, thus making the supervisee or mental health professional liable. In that circumstance, it is essential that consent to proceed with the proposed treatment be obtained from the client's legal representative who is authorized by law to give such consent.

Competency is related in some ways to understanding by the client, the second element necessary for valid informed consent. Information must be presented to clients in a way that enables them to understand the procedures to be used in counseling, what the risks and benefits of the counseling may be, and available alternative procedures. If a supervisee works with adolescents or children, the informed consent material should be explained on the minor's level, even though the ultimate decision for counseling rests with parents or legal guardians. There appears to be a growing trend in involving adolescents, especially, in the informed consent process regarding their counseling, and a majority of providers of psychotherapy feel that adolescents as young as 12 or 13 have the right to know important information about the therapeutic process. Research has indicated that including these minors in treatment decisions may facilitate the process, increase their psychological adjustment, and influence the results of their counseling (Adelman, Kaser-Boyd, & Taylor, 1984; Beeman & Scott, 1991; Weithorn, 1985).

In disclosing information to the client about treatment, the third element in valid informed consent, a question arises as to what and how much should be provided. Corey, Corey, and Callanan (1993) suggested that informed consent forms should contain general information about the therapeutic process, including possible disruptions that could take place in the client's life and goals of counseling; a fee schedule so that clients will be aware of their financial responsibility; some idea as to probable length of counseling; and information on alternatives to the type of counseling in which the client is about to engage.

The last of the four elements, voluntary consent, is the most straightforward of the necessary elements of informed consent. Voluntary consent means consent was given freely and not through any coercive means.

Haas (1991) elaborated on some of Corey, Corey, and Callanan's suggestions, noting that what necessary and sufficient informed consent consists of could be described briefly in seven categories. Two of Haas's seven categories address risks and benefits of treatment and alternative procedures. One of these risks of counseling could include embarrassment if other people know an individual is receiving counseling. Others may think that a person in counseling is not mentally stable. Another risk is that some people may experience distress when remembering unpleasant past experiences. The benefits of treatment usually include a higher level of functioning in a social, vocational, or family setting; fewer negative emotions; improved skill in succeeding at one's goals; and fewer self-defeating behaviors.

Logistics of treatment is a category that relates to the length of each counseling session and approximately how long treatment will go on (Haas, 1991). Cost of sessions and other services such as telephone consults, report writing, or handling of insurance should be included.

As much information as possible regarding the type of counseling used is important for professional counselors and supervisees to provide. For example, some supervisees may be behaviorally oriented and require clients, especially couples, to engage in homework assignments. Other supervisees may use the group approach and want clients not only to come to individual counseling but also attend additional group counseling sessions. In this category, preferred alternatives to the type of treatment offered as well as the risks of receiving no treatment at all should also be related to the client.

Emergency procedures are another category that should be addressed. "The therapist should have a backup or emergency service, and these arrangements should be described" (Haas, 1991, p. 184). For example, does the supervisee provide an after hours home phone number? Or does the supervisee prefer that clients call the supervisor or a crisis line at the local community health agency if a crisis should occur and the supervisee can not be reached? If a backup counselor other than the supervisor is used, confidentiality is compromised, and the client must be aware that the supervisee engages in this practice.

Haas's (1991) category of confidentiality in informed consent is imortant for supervisees to address. The client must know when confidentiality will be breached. The nature of the counselor's and supervisor's duties of confidentiality as well as the exceptions to confidentiality as discussed earlier must be explained to the client. Supervisees place themselves in a position to be sued for invasion of privacy and breach of confidentiality if they do not inform their clients that they will be discussing sessions with their supervisor. When clients are told by supervisees that information given in sessions will be discussed with the supervisor, trust is likely to be enhanced based on the supervisee's honesty. However, some clients of supervisees may be reluctant to reveal some types of personal information simply because there is a third party involved with whom the client has not established a trusting relationship. This can be avoided in one of several ways. Some supervisors address the issue by meeting with the supervisee and the client the first one or two sessions (Schuster, Sandt, & Thaler, 1972). This enables the client not only to be informed that a supervisor will be part of the therapeutic process but also enables the client to establish a limited relationship with the supervisor. Another method that helps avoid this problem is for the supervisor to meet periodically with the supervisee and the client.

Some psychotherapists trained in psychoanalysis feel that "the knowledge of a supervisor can lead to a formidable resistance or to splitting of the transference" (Cavenar, Rhoads, & Sullivan, 1980, p. 21). But even though psychoanalysts may feel that informing patients about supervisors will hinder the therapeutic process, they place themselves in a legally vulnerable position if they do not inform their clients initially, even if only once, that there is a supervisor involved.

The last important category in informed consent, according to Haas (1991), is qualifications of the provider. Usually this includes the provider's highest degree, specialty, or other services for which the clinician has had special training and experience. It should be made clear on the supervisee's informed consent statement for clients that the supervisee is either in training as a student counselor or is a counselor intern who has earned the master's degree and is working toward being licensed. Failure to accurately inform clients of the supervisee's status may expose both the supervisor and the supervisee to possible civil suits alleging claims of fraud, deceit, invasion of privacy, misrepresentation, lack of confidentiality, and lack of informed consent. Supervisees who are not licensed or otherwise credentialed and represent themselves as such to clients are taking a great risk. If sued, the court may hold them to the same standard of care as a credentialed professional, providing the same type of service is given. For example, in *Simpson v. Davis* (1976) a dentist who engaged in endodontic work was held to the same standard of care that would be expected of an endodontist. Even though this case involves dentistry, the same rule applies to medicine and mental health (*Cestone v. Harkavy*, 1935; *McBride v. United States*, 1972; *Rush v. Akron Hospital*, 1957).

A distinction should be made between unlicensed practitioners in states having licensing laws and those in states which do not. The general rule of law applicable to all professions is that an unlicensed practitioner alleged to have commited malpractice will be held to the same standard of care to which the licensed professional would be held in the same circumstance. However, in states where no licensing laws exist, the rule might be different. According to Harris (1973), an unlicensed mental health provider practicing in a state where no licensing law exists is likely to be subject to varying standards of care under different tort theories. Harris stated that "those people who practice outside the law are ... nonprofessionals not yet under the states' statutory umbrella. Since no standards are established for their reputed professions, someone injured by their 'care' will have to rely on tort theories other than malpractice" (pp. 408-409).

At one time, standard of care was determined by the professionals in a given locale. However, with improved communications and the availability of professional journals and continuing education courses, courts and legislatures have begun to hold professionals to a national standard of care (Ewing, 1985). If counselor interns or student counselors do not inform clients of their status, clients may assume these novice counselors have the general training and expertise expected of the typical professional in the field. The judicial system in each state may review the national standards for the professional counselor and hold supervisees to those standards if supervisees misrepresent themselves or render specialized services for which they have no training or are not otherwise qualified to provide.

The importance of providing clients of supervisees with thorough and accurate informed consent forms is clear. Mariano and Wolman (1986) stated that even though there is a balance to be sought in how much specific information regarding treatment should be disclosed to a client, the courts clearly favor disclosure rather than nondisclosure. It is important that the supervisee provide clients with information about background and the fact of supervision. This information in addition to details discussed by Corey, Corey, and Callanan (1993) and Haas (1991) should be placed in a readable informed consent form that is signed by both the client and the supervisee. Research has indicated that many psychologists in private practice do not use consent forms but prefer having oral agreements with their clients (Handelsman, Kemper, Kesson-Craig, McLain, & Johnsrud, 1986). However, using a signed form is one way for counselors to help supervisees prevail in suits of fraud, deceit, misrepresentation, invasion of privacy, breach of confidentiality, or lack of informed consent. The signed form is much more substantial as evidence in court than a simple verbal summary of informed consent elements and verbal consent on the part of the client.

Frequently Asked Questions

Q. If I am sued for something my supervisee did or failed to do, will my professional liability insurance cover me?

A. This question can be answered by checking the coverage statement on your professional liability insurance policy. For example, the coverage statement issued by RLI Insurance Company states that the insured is covered for any wrongful act by another person for whose actions the insured is legally responsible when those actions are performed on behalf of the insured and when those actions are performed as professional services for others in the same profession of the insured. This indicates that if the supervisor is sued based on negligent behavior of the supervisee, the supervisor's liability insurance is obligated to provide a defense for the supervisor. However, not all insurance companies provide the same coverage; for example, psychologists insured by American Home Assurance Company must purchase additional coverage for each person they supervise. It is recommended that the supervisor and supervisee purchase coverage from the same company or at least buy insurance on similar policy forms.

Q. I have been asked by several degreed counselor interns to supervise them as they meet the qualifications

for licensure. Even though I am an experienced licensed professional counselor myself, I have had no formal supervision training. If one of my supervisees became dissatisfied with my guidance and sued me for not providing adequate supervision, could the court see me as being incompetent?

A. Given that ACES has adopted standards for counseling supervisors, and formal training in supervision is part of those standards, the court indeed may consider you as supervisor incompetent. However, the generally accepted practices of those providing supervision for counselor interns is likely to be the most important consideration in the final decision by the judge or jury, and each case will stand on its own merit.

Q. I am a supervisor of five counseling practicum students. They have invited me to a party that one of the students is giving. Should I attend?

A. Both ethically and legally it is inadvisable for you as the supervisor to attend such a social event. This would constitute a dual relationship with supervisees. A sexual harassment charge is always a possibility if the supervisor's behavior is seen as, even in the most minimal way, improper. In order to avoid being liable for improper behaviors, it is best for supervisors to avoid all dual relationships with supervisees, even the seemingly innocuous ones.

Q. My supervisee is seeing a client who wants her insurance company to cover her fees. As the insurance company will not pay an unlicensed person, should I sign the form even though I am licensed but have never actually seen the client?

A. This is one of the most legally dangerous situations a counseling supervisor can face. Many insurance companies have filed fraud suits against therapists who sign off on their supervisees' client insurance forms when the supervisor never actually performed a service. The safest procedure to avoid prosecution is to note the professional relationship on the insurance form (i.e., "Jane Doe, MA, LPC, supervising counselor for John Jones, MA."). The counselor providing the service must sign the form as the service provider. The supervisor may also sign, indicating that he or she is providing supervision of the services provided by the counselor.

Q. I am employed as a licensed professional counselor in an agency setting and also supervise paraprofessional assistants hired by the agency. As part of the agency contract, due process is provided employees. In order to avoid having a suit brought against me for not following due process, what are some of the things that I need to do in regard to my supervisees?

A. The best defense when charged with violating due process requirements is to have all policies and expectations in writing as well as statements relating to the course of action that will be taken if the supervisee fails to abide by these policies. Specific requirements for successful employment and job performance should be addressed. These requirements should be operationally defined. This will lead to minimal ambiguity or prevent poor understanding on the part of the supervisee. Once the supervisee has read the requirements for successful performance, the supervisee should sign this paper indicating understanding and agreement. Additionally, any time the supervisee fails to perform in an acceptable fashion, the supervisor should not only confront the supervisee but also document the meetings where the unsatisfactory behavior was discussed. Consulting with another supervisor about the supervisee is also advisable. Even though the supervisee may sue the supervisor, regardless of appropriate due process behavior on the part of the supervisor, the supervisor will have a much better case if all due process requirements have been met during the supervisory relationship.

Guidelines for Practice

If you want to take steps to avoid being held legally responsible by clients for damages caused by your supervisee...

1. Develop informed consent forms with your supervisees, or review forms which the supervisees have developed independently, before allowing supervisees to have an initial session with a client.
2. If possible, meet with the client of the supervisee for the first one or two sessions. If this isn't possible, be sure that the supervisee informs clients that what is discussed in the therapeutic session will be reviewed with a supervisor.
3. Make sure the supervisee either audiotapes or videotapes sessions with clients and review every session, if possible, that supervisees have with clients.
4. If a client of one of your supervisees is experiencing a crisis situation, spend additional time in supervisory sessions with the supervisee.
5. Be prepared to meet with the supervisee and client during a session if there is any possibility that the supervisee may not be handling a client with the proper care.

If you want to be a clinical supervisor...

1. Check your state laws to see what qualifications you must have in order to be acceptable as a supervisor in your particular field.
2. If your state law requires training and experience, check with the state credentialing board to determine exactly what educational background and experiential requirements are necessary.
3. If your state laws do not have provisions concerning supervisor status, provide yourself with information regarding qualifications of other supervisors in your field to avoid having your competency questioned by the court in the event of a lawsuit. Make sure you possess at least the same or equal standards as those individuals. Be prepared to enroll in courses that are specifically related to supervision training.

To avoid potential liability of associates and assistants, if you are the main supervisor of a group of mental health workers you should...

1. Become thoroughly familiar with each supervisee's background including training and experience.
2. Do not assign any responsibilities to supervisees that they are not competent to perform.
3. Even if the supervisee appears to have training and experience in certain skills, closely supervise the supervisee initially in order to determine his or her level of expertise regarding this previous training and experience.
4. Meet with each supervisee at least once a week (or more) if the supervisee is a novice clinician or if the supervisee's client is in an emergency situation.
5. Do not supervise clinical activities for which you yourself do not have training or experience, such as supervising someone administering intelligence tests when you have had no formalized training in administration and interpretation of intelligence tests.

When you have been threatened or named as defendant in a civil suit brought by a client of one of your supervisees...

1. Do not panic.
2. Get in touch with your professional liability insurance agency and let them know that a lawsuit against you has been threatened or filed. The agency will appoint an attorney to represent you. The ACA program provides a toll-free hotline that allows those insured through ACA to consult with legal counsel immediately.
3. If you need additional legal advice, secure this on your own—and you will also have to pay for it yourself. Spend some time finding the best attorney to provide you with information. The most likely choice will be an attorney who has represented other mental health professionals in similar matters. If such an attorney is not available in your area, an attorney who represents physicians or similar professionals in malpractice situations should be the next choice. A third choice should be an attorney who has experience in domestic or family matters and who is interested in developing his or her knowledge and expertise regarding legal concerns of mental health professionals.
4. Set a time to meet with the attorney you have selected, and make a decision, once you have discussed the matter, whether the attorney will be an effective representative with your best interests in mind.
5. Provide the attorney with every detail that you have of the matter. Give truthful information.
6. Do not use your attorney as a counselor. If you are personally upset by this legal action, consult a colleague for support.

Summary

This monograph informs readers that few mental health care providers have been sued as they carried out their duties as clinical supervisors. However, the monograph also repeatedly warns that anyone may be sued at any time regardless of whether the litigant has a strong case. Therefore, all clinical supervisors must be familiar with the various aspects of the law that are related to their work. A proven wrongful act can make it impossible to get future liability insurance and could effectively ruin a career.

Many suggestions are provided to aid clinical supervisors in hopefully avoiding civil or criminal suits made against them. However, this monograph is only a general summary and not the last word on how clinical supervisors can protect themselves in a legal sense. The best course of action when legal questions arise is to seek advice from a qualified attorney. State laws that govern and license mental health workers vary, and therefore, getting legal advice from a qualified attorney in the clinical supervisor's community or state is always advisable.

Discussion Questions

1. What should be the limits of college supervisors interacting socially with practicum and intern students? Should specific guidelines for this interaction be established?

2. If a supervisor in an agency setting finds a supervisee failing to provide adequate care to clients, what steps should the supervisor take to remedy the situation? How can the supervisor reconcile the conflicting considerations regarding the duty to insure competent care to the client and to provide competent supervision with the economic consequences represented by the potential loss of income to the agency should the supervisee's clients be lost?

3. What is the proper clinical policy with regard to confidentiality and record keeping in the process of supervision? Which specific items are considered client materials and are required by law to remain confidential? (For a broad discussion of confidentiality issues, see C*onfidentiality and Privileged Communication,* Volume 6 in the ACA Legal Series, by Gibbs L. Arthur, Jr., and Carl D. Swanson.)

4. What are possible legal consequences of breaching confidentiality when not required by law to do so? What are possible legal consequences of refusing to reveal confidential informa-

tion when required by law to do so? (For a discussion of the circumstances in which the supervisor/counselor is required by law to reveal otherwise confidential client information, also see *Confidentiality and Privileged Communication.*)

5. How will the courts determine the issue of a supervisor's competence? What standards will be used in assessing competence? What factors will be considered in determining whether the standard of competence was breached in each individual case before the court?

6. What clinical policies should be established for notification of supervisees of the required level of skill and competence for successful completion of the practicum or internship? What policy should be established for the ongoing review and evaluation of the supervisee's performance? What policy should be established for informing the supervisee that the performance is unacceptable and for attempting to resolve areas of deficiency? At what point is it proper to dismiss the supervisee from the practicum or internship? What procedure for terminating the supervisee must be followed in order to avoid violating the supervisee's due process rights?

Suggested Readings

Arthur, G. L., Jr., & Swanson, C.D. (1993). *Confidentiality and privileged communication* (ACA Legal Series, Vol. 6). Alexandria, VA: American Counseling Association. Contains a thorough discussion of confidentiality and privileged communication in a legal framework.

Borders, L.D., & Leddick, G.R. (1987). *Handbook of counseling supervision*. Alexandria, VA: Association for Counselor Education and Supervision. Provides specific guidelines for those in a supervisory position. Contains a supervisor rating scale to be completed by supervisees that could be used to indicate supervisor competence.

Cohen, R.J., & Mariano, W.E. (1982). *Legal guidebook in mental health*. New York: Free Press. Provides a general summary of many issues addressed in this monograph and other legal issues in the helping professions.

Corey, G., Corey, M.S., & Callanan P. (1993). *Issues and ethics in the helping professions* (4th ed.) Pacific Grove, CA: Brooks/Cole. Provides an indepth discussion on ethical issues and how many of these issues relate to legal concerns. Contains many pertinent references.

Fischer, L., & Sorenson, G.P. (1985). *School law for counselors, psychologists, and social workers*. New York: Longman. Covers many topics of a legal nature specifically of interest to school counselors and those who supervise school counselors.

Vesper, J.H., & Brock, G.W. (1991). *Ethics, legalities, and professional practice issues in marriage and family therapy*. Boston: Allyn & Bacon. Contains information related to legal concerns of marriage and family counselors. Provides specific information on supervision such as legal liability and supervising in educational settings.

Woody, R.H. (1988). *Fifty ways to avoid malpractice: A guideline for mental health professionals*. Sarasota, FL: Professional Resource Exchange. Provides a general guide on steps to take to avoid malpractice suits. Discusses vicarious liability, standards of care, and negligence.

References

Adelman, H.S., Kaser-Boyd, N., & Taylor, L. (1984). Children's participation in consent for psychotherapy and their subsequent response to treatment. *Journal of Clinical Child Psychology, 13*, 170-178.

American Association for Marriage and Family Therapy. (1988). *Code of ethical principles for marriage and family therapists.* Washington, DC: Author.

Association for Counselor Education and Supervision. (1989). *Standards for counseling supervisors.* Alexandria, VA: American Association for Counseling and Development.

Association for Counselor Education and Supervision. (1993). *Ethical guidelines for counseling supervisors.* Alexandria, VA: Author.

American Psychological Association. (1992). *Ethical principles of psychologists and code of conduct.* Washington, D.C.: Author.

Bartell, P.A., & Rubin, L.J. (1990). Dangerous liaisons: Sexual intimacies in supervision. *Professional Psychology: Research and Practice, 21*, 442-450.

Beeman, D.G., & Scott, N.A. (1991). Therapists' attitudes toward psychotherapy informed consent with adolescents. *Professional Psychology: Research and Practice, 22* (3), 230-234.

Bernard, J.M. (1979). Supervisory training: A discrimination model. *Counselor Education and Supervision, 19*, 60-68.

Bernard, J.M. (1981). Inservice training for clinical supervisors. *Professional Psychology: Research and Practice, 12*, 740-748.

Bernard, J.L., & O'Laughlin, D.L. (1990). Confidentiality: Do training clinics take it seriously? *Law & Psychology Review, 14* (59), 59-69.

Black's Law Dictionary (6th ed.). (1990). St. Paul, MN: West.

Board of Medical Quality Assurance, Psychology Examining Committee, State of California Department of Consumer Affairs. (1977, September 10). *Order adopting, amending, and repealing regulations of the Board of Medical Quality Assurance, Psychology Examining Committee.* Sacramento, CA: Author.

Borders, L.D. (1983, October). *Supervising the novice supervisor.* Paper presented at the Southern Association for Counselor Education and Supervision, Mobile, AL.

Borders, L.D. (1986). Facilitating supervisee growth: Implications of developmental models of counseling supervision. *Michigan Journal of Counseling and Development, 19*, 129-136.

Borders, L.D., & Leddick, G.R. (1987). *Handbook of counseling supervision.* Alexandria, VA: Association for Counselor Education and Supervision.

Bradley, L. (1989). *Counselor supervision.* Muncie,IN: Accelerated Development.

Burlew, L.D., Emerson, P., Disney, J., Folse, E., Roland, C., & Benshoff, J. (1992). *Counseling supervisory training: A workbook.* Dubuque, IA: Kendall/ Hunt.

Cavenar, J., Rhoads, E., & Sullivan, J. (1980). Ethical and legal aspects of supervision. *Bulletin of the Menninger Clinic, 44*, 15-22.

Cestone v. Harkavy, 243 App. Div. 732, 277 N.Y.S.2d 438 (1935).

Connelly v. University of Vermont and State Agricultural College, 244 F.Supp. 156 (D Vt. 1965).

Corey, G., Corey, M.S., & Callanan, P. (1993). *Issues and ethics in the helping professions* (4th ed.) Pacific Grove, CA: Brooks/ Cole.

Cormier, L.S., & Bernard, J.M. (1982). Ethical and legal responsibilities of clinical supervisors. *Personnel and Guidance Journal, 60*, 486-491.

Cross, D.G., & Brown, D. (1983). Counselor supervision as a function of trainee experience: Analysis of specific behaviors. *Counselor Education and Supervision, 22*, 333-341.

Dixon v. Alabama State Board of Education, 294 F.2d 150 (5th Cir.) cert. denied, 368 U.S. 930 (1961).

Ewing, C.P. (Ed.). (1985). *Psychology, psychiatry, and the law: A clinical and forensic handbook.* Sarasota, FL: Professional Resource Exchange.

Felthous, A.R. (1989). The ever confusing jurisprudence of the psychotherapist's duty to protect. *Journal of Psychiatry and Law*, Winter, 575-594.

Fla. Stat. Ann. Sec 491.005, 1987.

Ga. Code Ann. Sec 43-10a-3 (Supp. 1991).

Gaspar v. Bruton, 513 F.2d 843 (CA 10 1975).

Glaser, R.D., & Thorpe, J.S. (1986). Unethical intimacy: A survey of sexual contact and advances between psychology educators and female graduate students. *American Psychologist, 41* (1), 43-51.

Goss v. Lopez, 419 U.S. 565 (1975).

Greenhill v. Bailey, 519 F.2d 5 (8th Cir. 1975).

Haas, L.J. (1991). Hide-and-seek or show-and-tell? Emerging issues of informed consent. *Ethics and Behavior, 1* (3), 175-189.

Handelsman, M.M., Kemper, M.B., Kesson-Craig, P., McLain, J., & Johnsrud, C. (1986). Use, consent, and readability of written informed consent forms for treatment. *Professional Psychology: Research and Practice, 17*, 514-518.

Harris, M. (1973). Tort liability of the psychotherapist. *University of San Francisco Law Review, 8*, 405-436.

Hart, G. (1982). *The process of clinical supervision.* Baltimore: University Park Press.

Heppner, P.P., & Roehlke, H.J. (1984). Differences among supervisees at different levels of training: Implications for a developmental model of training. *Journal of Counseling Psychology, 31*, 76-90.

Hess, A.K. (Ed.). (1980). *Psychotherapy supervision: Theory, research, and practice.* New York: Wiley.

Hess, A.K., & Hess, K.A. (1983). Psychotherapy supervision: A survey of internship training practices. *Professional Psychology: Research and Practice, 14* (4), 504-513.

Hess, A.K. (1987). Psychotherapy supervision: Stages, Buber, and a theory of relationship. *Professional Psychology: Research and Practice, 18*, 251-259.

Jennings, E.K. (1981). Breach of contract suits by students against postsecondary institutions: Can they succeed? *Journal of College and University Law, 7*(3-4), 191-221.

Kapp, M.B. (1981). Legal issues in faculty evaluation of student clinical performance. *Journal of Medical Education, 56*, 559-564.

Knoff, H.M., & Prout, H.T. (1985). Terminating students from professional psychology programs: Criteria, procedures, and legal issues. *Professional Psychology: Research and Practice, 16*, 789-797.

Littrell, J.M., Lee-Borden, N., & Lorenz, J. (1979). A developmental framework for counseling supervision. *Counselor Education and Supervision, 19*, 129-136.

Loganbill, C., Hardy, E., & Delworth, U. (1982). Supervision: A conceptual model. *The Consulting Psychologist, 10*(1), 3-42.

Mariano, W.E., & Wolman, D. (1986). Boundaries between the law and behavior therapies. In L. Everstine & D.S. Everstine (Eds.), *Psychotherapy and the Law* (pp. 267-277). Orlando, FL: Grune & Stratton.

Markowitz, M. (1958). A supervisor supervised: A subjective eclective experience. *American Journal of Psychotherapy, 12*, 488-492.

McAfee, J.K., & Cote, L.S. (1985). Avoid having your day in court. *Training and Development Journal, 39* (4), 56-60.

McBride v. United States, 462 f.2d 72(9 Cir. 1972).

Miles, A.S. (1987). The due process rights of students in public school or college disciplinary hearings. *The Alabama Lawyer, 48* (3), 144-146.

Neukrug, E.S., Healy, M., & Herlihy, B. (1992). Ethical practices of licensed professional counselors: An updated survey of state licensing boards. *Counselor Education and Supervision, 32*(2), 81-176.

Newman, A.S. (1981). Ethical issues in the supervision of psychotherapy. *Professional Psychology: Research and Practice, 12*, 690-695.

Pope, K.S., Levenson, H., & Schover, L.R. (1979). Sexual intimacy in psychology training: Results and implications of a national survey. *American Psychologist, 34*, 682-689.

Pope, K., Schover, L., & Levenson, H. (1980). Sexual behavior between clinical supervisors and trainees: Implications for professional standards. *Professional Psychology: Research and Practice, 10*, 278-284.

Robiner, W.N., Fuhrman, M.J., & Bobbitt, B.L. (1990). Supervision in the practice of psychology: Toward the development of a supervisory instrument. *Psychotherapy in Private Practice, 8* (1), 87-98.

Rush v. Akron Hospital, 171 NE2d 378 (Ohio App. 1957).

S.C. Code Ann. Sec 40-75-105 (Supp. 1991).

Schuster, D.B., Sandt, J.J., & Thaler, O.F. (1972). *Clinical supervision of the psychiatric resident*. New York: Brunner/Mazel.

Shuffer v. Trustees of California State University and Colleges, 136 Cal.Rptr. 527 (1977).

Simpson v. Davis, 219 Kan.584, 549 P.2d 950 (1976).

Stenack, R., & Dye, H. (1982). Behavioral descriptions of counseling supervision roles. *Counselor Education and Supervision, 21*, 295-304.

Stoltenberg, C. (1981). Approaching supervision from a developmental perspective: The counselor complexity model. *Journal of Counseling Psychology, 28*, 59-65.

Stoltenberg, C.D., & Delworth, U. (1987). *Supervising counselors and therapists*. San Francisco: Jossey-Bass.

Stromberg, C., Haggarty, D., Leibenluft, R., McMillian, M., Mishkin, B., Rubin, B., & Trilling, H. (1988). *The psychologist's legal handbook*. Washington, DC: Council for the National Register of Health Service Providers in Psychology.

Tarasoff v. Regents of the University of California, 131 Cal. Rptr. 14, 551 P. 2d. 334 (1976).

Vesper, J.H., & Brock, G.W. (1991). *Ethics, legalities, and professional practice issues in marriage and family therapy*. Boston: Allyn & Bacon.

Van Look v. Curran, 489 So 2nd 525, 528 (Ala. 1986).

Weithorn, L.A. (1985). Children's capacities for participation in treatment decision-making. In D.H. Schetzky & E.P. Benedek (Eds.), *Emerging issues in child psychiatry and the law* (pp. 22-36). New York: Brunner/Mazel.

Wilkinson, A.P. (1982). Psychiatric malpractice: Identifying areas of liability. *Trial, 18*, 73-77.

Woody, R.H. (1985). Public policy, malpractice law, and the mental health professional: Some legal and clinical guidelines. In C. P. Ewing (Ed.), *Psychology, psychiatry, and the law: A clinical and forensic handbook* (pp. 509-525). Sarasota, FL: Professional Resource Exchange.

Zipkin v. Freeman, 436 S.W.2d 753 at 761 (Supp.ct., Mo. 1969).

Appendix A

Ethical Guidelines for Counseling Supervisors

Preamble

The Association for Counselor Education and Supervision (ACES) is composed of people engaged in the professional preparation of counselors and people responsible for the ongoing supervision of counselors. ACES is a founding division of the American Counseling Association (ACA) and as such adheres to ACA's current ethical standards and to general codes of competence adopted throughout the mental health community.

ACES believes that counselor educators and counseling supervisors in universities and in applied counseling settings, including the range of education and mental health delivery systems, carry responsibilities unique to their job roles. Such responsibilities may include administrative supervision, clinical supervision, or both. Administrative supervision refers to those supervisory activities which increase the efficiency of the delivery of counseling services; whereas, clinical supervision includes the supportive and educative activities of the supervisor designed to improve the application of counseling theory and technique directly to clients.

Counselor educators and counseling supervisors encounter situations which challenge the help given by general ethical standards of the profession at large. These situations require more specific guidelines that provide appropriate guidance in everyday practice.

The Ethical Guidelines for Counseling Supervisors are intended to assist professionals by helping them:

1. observe ethical and legal protection of clients' and supervisees' rights;
2. meet the training and professional development needs of supervisees in ways consistent with clients' welfare and programmatic requirements; and
3. establish policies, procedures, and standards for implementing programs.

The specification of ethical guidelines enables ACES members to focus on and to clarify the ethical nature of responsibilities held in common. Such guidelines should be reviewed formally every 5 years, or more often if needed, to meet the needs of ACES members for guidance.

The Ethical Guidelines for Counselor Educators and Counseling Supervisors are meant to help ACES members in conducting supervision. ACES is not currently in a position to hear complaints about alleged noncompliance with these guidelines. Any complaints about the ethical behavior of any ACA member should be measured against the ACA Ethical Standards and a complaint lodged with ACA in accordance with their procedures for doing so.

One overriding assumption underlying this document is that supervision should be ongoing throughout a counselor's career and not stop when a particular level of education, certification, or membership in a professional organization is attained.

Definitions of Terms:

Applied Counseling Settings—Public or private organizations of counselors such as community mental health centers, hospitals, schools, and group or individual private practice settings.

Supervisees—Counselors-in-training in university programs at any level who are working with clients in applied settings as part of their university training program, and counselors who have completed their formal education and are employed in an applied counseling setting.

Supervisors—Counselors who have been designated within their university or agency to directly oversee the professional clinical work of counselors. Supervisors also may be persons who offer supervision to counselors seeking state licensure and so provide supervision outside of the administrative aegis of an applied counseling setting.

1. Client Welfare and Rights

1.01 The primary obligation of supervisors is to train counselors so that they respect the integrity and promote the welfare of their clients. Supervisors should have supervisees inform clients that they are being supervised and that observation and/or recordings of the session may be reviewed by the supervisor.

1.02 Supervisors who are licensed counselors and are conducting supervision to aid a supervisee to become licensed should instruct the supervisee not to communicate or in any way convey to the supervisee's clients or to other parties that the supervisee is himself/herself licensed.

1.03 Supervisors should make supervisees aware of clients' rights, including protecting clients' right to privacy and confidentiality in the counseling relationship and the information resulting from it. Clients also should be informed that their right to privacy and confidentiality will not be violated by the supervisory relationship.

1.04 Records of the counseling relationship, including interview notes, test data, correspondence, the electronic storage of these documents, and audio- and videotape recordings are considered to be confidential professional information. Supervisors should see that these materials are used in counseling, research, and training and supervision of counselors with the full knowledge of the client and that permission to use these materials is granted by the applied counseling setting offering service to the client. This professional information is to be used for the full protection of the client. Written consent from the client (or legal guardian, if a minor) should be secured prior to the use of such information for instructional, supervisory, and/or research purposes. Policies of the applied counseling setting regarding client records also should be followed.

1.05 Supervisors shall adhere to current professional and legal guidelines when conducting research with human participants such as Section D-1 of the ACA Ethical Standards.

1.06 Counseling supervisors are responsible for making every effort to monitor both the professional actions, and failures to take action, of their supervisees.

2. Supervisory Role

Inherent and integral to the role of supervisor are responsibilities for:

a. monitoring client welfare;
b. encouraging compliance with relevant legal, ethical, and professional standards for clinical practice;
c. monitoring clinical performance and professional development of supervisees; and
d. evaluating and certifying current performance and potential of supervisees for academic, screening, selection, placement, employment, and credentialing purposes.

2.01 Supervisors should have had training in supervision prior to initiating their role as supervisors.

2.02 Supervisors should pursue professional and personal continuing education activities such as advanced courses, seminars, and professional conferences on a regular and ongoing basis. These activities should include both counseling and supervision topics and skills.

2.03 Supervisors should make their supervisees aware of professional and ethical standards and legal responsibilities of the counseling profession.

2.04 Supervisors of postdegree counselors who are seeking state licensure should encourage these counselors to adhere to the standards for practice established by the state licensure board of the state in which they practice.

2.05 Procedures for contacting the supervisor, or an alternative supervisor, to assist in handling crisis situations should be established and communicated to supervisees.

2.06 Actual work samples via audio and/or video tape or live observation in addition to case notes should be reviewed by the supervisor as a regular part of the ongoing supervisory process.

2.07 Supervisors of counselors should meet regularly in face-to-face sessions with their supervisees.

2.08 Supervisors should provide supervisees with ongoing feedback on their performance. This feedback should take a variety of forms, both formal and informal, and should include verbal and written evaluations. It should be formative during the supervisory experience and summative at the conclusion of the experience.

2.09 Supervisors who have multiple roles (e.g., teacher, clinical supervisor, administrative supervisor, etc.) with supervisees should minimize potential conflicts. Where possible, the roles should be divided among several supervisors. Where this is not possible, careful explanation should be conveyed to the supervisee as to the expectations and responsibilities associated with each supervisory role.

2.10 Supervisors should not participate in any form of sexual contact with supervisees. Supervisors should not engage in any form of social contact or interaction which would compromise the supervisor-supervisee relationship. Dual relationships with supervisees that might impair the supervisor's objectivity and professional judgment should be avoided and/or the supervisory relationship terminated.

2.11 Supervisors should not establish a psychotherapeutic relationship as a substitute for supervision. Personal issues should be addressed in supervision only in terms of the impact of these issues on clients and on professional functioning.

2.12 Supervisors, through ongoing supervisee assessment and evaluation, should be aware of any personal or professional limitations of supervisees which are likely to impede future professional performance. Supervisors have the responsibility of recommending remedial assistance to the supervisee and of screening from the training program, applied counseling setting, or state licensure those supervisees who are unable to provide competent professional services. These recommendations should be clearly and professionally explained in writing to the supervisees who are so evaluated.

2.13 Supervisors should not endorse a supervisee for certification, licensure, completion of an academic training program, or continued employment if the supervisor believes the supervisee is impaired in any way that would interfere with the performance of counseling duties. The presence of any such impairment should begin a process of feedback and remediation wherever possible so that the supervisee understands the nature of the impairment and has the opportunity to remedy the problem *and* continue with his/her professional development.

2.14 Supervisors should incorporate the principles of informed consent and participation; clarity of requirements, expectations, roles and rules; and due process and appeal into the establishment of policies and procedures of their institution, program, courses, and individual supervisory relationships. Mechanisms for due process appeal of individual supervisory actions should be established and made available to all supervisees.

3. **Program Administration Role**

3.01 Supervisors should ensure that the programs conducted and experiences provided are in keeping with current guidelines and standards of ACA and its divisions.

3.02 Supervisors should teach courses and/or supervise clinical work only in areas where they are fully competent and experienced.

3.03 To achieve the highest quality of training and supervision, supervisors should be active participants in peer review and peer supervision procedures.

3.04 Supervisors should provide experiences that integrate theoretical knowledge and practical application. Supervisors also should provide opportunities in which supervisees are able to apply the knowledge they have learned and understand the rationale for the skills they have acquired. The knowledge and skills conveyed should reflect current practice, research findings, and available resources.

3.05 Professional competencies, specific courses, and/or required experiences expected of supervisees should be communicated to them in writing prior to admission to the training program or placement/employment by the applied counseling setting, and, in the case of continued employment, in a timely manner.

3.06 Supervisors should accept only those persons as supervisees who meet identified entry level requirements for admission to a program of counselor training or for placement in an applied counseling setting. In the case of private supervision in search of state licensure, supervisees should have completed all necessary prerequisites as determined by the state licensure board.

3.07 Supervisors should inform supervisees of the goals, policies, theoretical orientations toward counseling, training, and supervision model or approach on which the supervision is based.

3.08 Supervisees should be encouraged and assisted to define their own theoretical orientation toward counseling, to establish supervision goals for themselves, and to monitor and evaluate their progress toward meeting these goals.

3.09 Supervisors should assess supervisees' skills and experience in order to establish standards for competent professional behavior. Supervisors should restrict supervisees' activities to those that are commensurate with their current level of skills and experiences.

3.10 Supervisors should obtain practicum and fieldwork sites that meet minimum standards for preparing students to become effective counselors. No practicum or fieldwork setting should be approved unless it truly replicates a counseling work setting.

3.11 Practicum and fieldwork classes should be limited in size according to established professional standards to ensure that each student has ample opportunity for individual supervision and feedback. Supervisors in applied counseling settings should have a limited number of supervisees.

3.12 Supervisors in university settings should establish and communicate specific policies and procedures regarding field placement of students. The respective roles of the student counselor, the university supervisor, and the field supervisor should be clearly differentiated in areas such as evaluation, requirements, and confidentiality.

3.13 Supervisors in training programs should communicate regularly with supervisors in agencies used as practicum and/or fieldwork sites regarding current professional practices, expectations of students, and preferred models and modalities of supervision.

3.14 Supervisors at the university should establish clear lines of communication among themselves, the field supervisors, and the students/supervisees.

3.15 Supervisors should establish and communicate to supervisees and to field supervisors specific procedures regarding consultation, performance review, and evaluation of supervisees.

3.16 Evaluations of supervisee performance in universities and in applied counseling settings should be available to supervisees in ways consistent with the Family Rights and Privacy Act and the Buckley Amendment.

3.17 Forms of training that focus primarily on self-understanding and problem resolution (e.g., personal growth groups or individual counseling) should be voluntary. Those who conduct these forms of training should not serve simultaneously as supervisors of the supervisees involved in the training.

3.18 A supervisor may recommend participation in activities such as personal growth groups or personal counseling when it has been determined that a supervisee has deficits in the areas of self-understanding and problem resolution which impede his/her professional functioning. The supervisor should not be the direct provider of these activities for the supervisee.

3.19 When a training program conducts a personal growth or counseling experience involving relatively intimate self- disclosure, care should be taken to eliminate or minimize potential role conflicts for faculty and/or agency supervisors who may conduct these experiences and who also serve as teachers, group leaders, and clinical directors.

3.20 Supervisors should use the following prioritized sequence in resolving conflicts among the needs of the client, the needs of the supervisee, and the needs of the program or agency. Insofar as the client must be protected, it should be understood that client welfare is usually subsumed in federal and state laws such that these statutes should be the first point of reference. Where laws and ethical standards are not present or are unclear, the good judgment of the supervisor should be guided by the following list:

a. relevant legal and ethical standards (e.g. duty to warn, state child abuse laws, etc.);
b. client welfare;
c. supervisee welfare;
d. supervisor welfare; and
e. program and/or agency service and administrative needs.

Appendix B

Standards for Counseling Supervisors

Supervision Interest Network, Association for Counselor Education and Supervision

(As adopted by the AACD Governing Council, July 13–16, 1989)

The standards include a description of 11 core areas of personal traits, knowledge, and competencies that are characteristic of effective supervisors. The level of preparation and experience of the counselor, the particular work setting of the supervisor and counselor, and client variables will influence the relative emphasis of each competency in practice.

These core areas and their related competencies have been consistently identified in supervision research and, in addition, have been judged to have face validity as determined by supervisor practitioners, based on both select and widespread peer review.

1. Professional counseling supervisors are *effective counselors* whose knowledge and competencies have been acquired through training, education, and supervised employment experience. The counseling supervisor:

1.1 demonstrates knowledge of various counseling theories, systems, and their related methods;
1.2 demonstrates knowledge of his/her personal philosophical, theoretical, and methodological approach to counseling;
1.3 demonstrates knowledge of his/her assumptions about human behavior; and
1.4 demonstrates skill in the application of counseling theory and methods (individual, group, or marital and family and specialized areas such as substance abuse, career-life rehabilitation) that are appropriate for the supervisory setting.

2. Professional counseling supervisors demonstrate *personal traits and characteristics* that are consistent with the role. The counseling supervisor:

2.1 is committed to updating his/her own counseling and supervisory skills;
2.2 is sensitive to individual differences;
2.3 recognizes his/her own limits through self-evaluation and feedback from others;
2.4 is encouraging, optimistic, and motivational;
2.5 possesses a sense of humor;
2.6 is comfortable with the authority inherent in the role of supervisor;
2.7 demonstrates a commitment to the role of supervisor;
2.8 can identify his/her own strengths and weaknesses as a supervisor; and
2.9 can describe his/her own pattern in interpersonal relationships.

3. Professional counseling supervisors are knowledgeable regarding *ethical, legal, and regulatory aspects* of the professional, and are skilled in applying this knowledge. The counseling supervisor:

3.1 communicates to the counselor a knowledge of professional codes of ethics (e.g., AACD, APA);
3.2 demonstrates and enforces ethical and professional standards;

3.3 communicates to the counselor an understanding of legal and regulatory documents and their impact on the profession (e.g., certification, licensure, duty to warn, parents' rights to children's records, third-party payments, etc.);
3.4 provides current information regarding professional standards (NCC, CCMHC, CRC, CCC, licensure, certification, etc.);
3.5 can communicate a knowledge of counselor rights and appeal procedures specific to the work setting; and
3.6 communicates to the counselor a knowledge of ethical considerations that pertain to the supervisory process, including dual relationships, due process, evaluation, informed consent, confidentiality, and vicarious liability.

4. Professional counseling supervisors demonstrate conceptual knowledge of the *personal and professional nature of the supervisory relationship* and are skilled in applying this knowledge.
The counseling supervisor:

4.1 demonstrates knowledge of individual differences with respect to gender, race ethnicity, culture, and age and understands the importance of these characteristics in supervisory relationships;
4.2 is sensitive to the counselor's personal and professional needs;
4.3 expects counselors to own the consequences of their actions;
4.4 is sensitive to the evaluative nature of supervision and effectively responds to the counselor's anxiety relative to performance evaluation;
4.5 conducts self-evaluations, as appropriate, as a means of modeling professional growth;
4.6 provides facilitative conditions (empathy, concreteness, respect, congruence, genuineness, and immediacy);
4.7 establishes a mutually trusting relationship with the counselor;
4.8 provides an appropriate balance of challenge and support; and

4.9 elicits counselor thoughts and feelings during counseling or consultation sessions, and responds in a manner that enhances the supervision process.

5. Professional counseling supervisors demonstrate conceptual knowledge of *supervision methods and techniques*, and are skilled in using this knowledge to promote counselor development.

The counseling supervisor:

5.1 states the purposes of supervision and explains the procedures to be used;
5.2 negotiates mutual decisions regarding the needed direction of learning experiences for the counselor;
5.3 engages in appropriate supervisory interventions, including role play, role reversal, live supervision, modeling, interpersonal process recall, micro training, suggestions and advice, reviewing audio- and videotapes, etc.;
5.4 can perform the supervisor's functions in the role of teacher, counselor, or consultant as appropriate;
5.5 elicits new alternatives from counselors for identifying solutions, techniques, responses to clients;
5.6 integrates knowledge of supervision with his/her style of interpersonal relations;
5.7 clarifies his/her role in supervision;
5.8 uses media aids (print material, electronic recording) to enhance learning; and
5.9 interacts with the counselor in a manner that facilitates the counselor's self-exploration and problem solving.

6. Professional counseling supervisors demonstrate conceptual knowledge of the *counselor developmental process* and are skilled in applying this knowledge.

The counseling supervisor:

6.1 understands the developmental nature of supervision;
6.2 demonstrates knowledge of various theoretical models of supervision;

6.3 understands the counselor's roles and functions in particular work settings;
6.4 understands the supervisor's roles and functions in particular work settings;
6.5 can identify the learning needs of the counselor;
6.6 adjusts conference content based on the counselor's personal traits, conceptual development, training, and experience; and
6.7 uses supervisory methods appropriate to the counselor's level of conceptual development, training, and experience.

7. Professional counseling supervisors demonstrate knowledge and competency in *case conceptualization and management.* The counseling supervisor:

7.1 recognizes that a primary goal of supervision is helping the client of the counselor;
7.2 understands the roles of other professionals (e.g., psychologists, physicians, social workers) and assists with the referral process, when appropriate;
7.3 elicits counselor perceptions of counseling dynamics;
7.4 assists the counselor in selecting and executing data collection procedures;
7.5 assists the counselor in analyzing and interpreting data objectively;
7.6 assists the counselor in planning effective client goals and objectives;
7.7 assists the counselor in using observation and assessment in preparation of client goals and objectives;
7.8 assists the counselor in synthesizing client psychological and behavioral characteristics into an integrated conceptualization;
7.9 assists the counselor in assigning priorities to counseling goals and objectives;
7.10 assists the counselor in providing rationale for counseling procedures; and
7.11 assists the counselor in adjusting steps in the progession toward a goal based on ongoing assessment and evaluation.

8. Professional counseling supervisors demonstrate knowledge and competency in client *assessment and evaluation.* The counseling supervisor:

   8.1 monitors the use of tests and test interpretations;
   8.2 assists the counselor in providing rationale for assessment procedures;
   8.3 assists the counselor in communicating assessment procedures and rationales;
   8.4 assists the counselor in the description, measurement, and documentation of client and counselor change; and
   8.5 assists the counselor in integrating findings and observations to make appropriate recommendations.

9. Professional counseling supervisors demonstrate knowledge and competency in *oral and written reporting and recording.* The counseling supervisor:

   9.1 understands the meaning of accountability and the supervisor's responsibility in promoting it;
   9.2 assists the counselor in effectively documenting supervisory and counseling-related interactions;
   9.3 assists the counselor in establishing and following policies and procedures to protect the confidentiality of client and supervisory records;
   9.4 assists the counselor in identifying appropriate information to be included in a verbal or written report;
   9.5 assists the counselor in presenting information in a logical, concise, and sequential manner; and
   9.6 assists the counselor in adapting verbal and written reports to the work environment and communication situation.

10. Professional counseling supervisors demonstrate knowledge and competency in the *evaluation of counseling performance.* The counseling supervisor:

   10.1 can interact with the counselor from the perspective of evaluator;

10.2 can identify the counselor's professional and personal strengths, as well as weaknesses;
10.3 provides specific feedback about such performance as conceptualization, use of methods and techniques, relationship skills, and assessment;
10.4 determines the extent to which the counselor has developed and applied his/her own personal theory of counseling;
10.5 develops evaluation procedures and instruments to determine program and counselor goal attainment;
10.6 assists the counselor in the description and measurement of his/her progress and achievement; and
10.7 can evaluate counseling skills for purposes of grade assignment, completion of internship requirements, professional advancement, and so on.

11. Professional counseling supervisors are knowledgeable regarding *research in counseling and counselor supervision* and consistently incorporate this knowledge into the supervision process.
The counseling supervisor:

11.1 facilitates and monitors research to determine the effectiveness of programs, services, and techniques;
11.2 reads, interprets, and applies counseling and supervisory research;
11.3 can formulate counseling or supervisory research questions;
11.4 reports results of counseling or supervisory research and disseminates as appropriate (e.g., inservice, conferences, publications); and
11.5 facilitates an integration of research findings in individual case management.

The Education and Training of Supervisors

Counseling supervision is a distinct field of preparation and practice. Knowledge and competencies necessary for effective performance are acquired through a sequence of training and experience which ordinarily includes the following:

1. graduate training in counseling;
2. successful supervised employment as a professional counselor;
3. credentialing in one or more of the following areas: certification by a state department of education, licensure by a state as a professional counselor, and certification as a National Certified Counselor, Certified Clinical Mental Health Counselor, Certified Rehabilitation Counselor, or Certified Career Counselor;
4. graduate training in counseling supervision including didactic courses, seminars, laboratory courses, and supervision practica;
5. continuing educational experiences specific to supervision theory and practice (e.g., conferences, workshops, self-study); and
6. research activities related to supervision theory and practice.

The supervisor's primary functions are to teach the inexperienced and to foster their professional development, to serve as consultants to experienced counselors, and to assist at all levels in the provision of effective counseling services. These responsibilities require personal and professional maturity accompanied by a broad perspective on counseling that is gained by extensive, supervised counseling experience. Therefore, training for supervision generally occurs during advanced graduate study or continuing professional development. This is not to say, however, that supervisor training in the preservice stage is without merit. The presentation of basic methods and procedures may enhance students' performance as counselors, enrich their participation in the supervision process, and provide a framework for later study.